PROSPERITY AND VIOLENCE

PROSPERITY

AND

VIOLENCE

THE POLITICAL ECONOMY

OF DEVELOPMENT

ROBERT H. BATES

W. W. NORTON & COMPANY

NEW YORK • LONDON

The text of this book is composed in Garamond 3
with the display set in Engravers Bold
Composition by Tom Ernst
Manufacturing by Quebecor Fairfield

Library of Congress Cataloging-in-Publication Data

Bates, Robert H.
Prosperity and violence : the political economy of development /
by Robert H. Bates.
p.   cm.
Includes bibliographical references and index.
ISBN 0-393-05038-6
1. Economic development. 2. Social policy. 3. Violence. I. Title.

HD82.B3257 2001
338.9—dc21   00-056608

W. W. Norton & Company, Inc., 500 Fifth Avenue, New York, N.Y. 10110
www.wwnorton.com

W. W. Norton & Company Ltd., 10 Coptic Street, London WC1A 1PU

1 2 3 4 5 6 7 8 9 0

To Helen McClimans and Joseph T. Rouse, Senior

CONTENTS

LIST OF FIGURES

ACKNOWLEDGMENTS

THE ROOTS OF THIS BOOK draw nourishment from my membership in several academic communities, my experiences with students, and the research I have conducted in the field.

While preparing for fieldwork in Africa, I studied social anthropology at the University of Manchester. Diverse fields of learning—sociology, history, and economics—poured into the debates that filled the corridors of Manchester's Department of Sociology and Social Anthropology; influential books, articles, and polemics poured out. Interdisciplinary work took place in an environment in which no ideas were barred or spared keen scrutiny. The spirit of that department has long influenced my thinking and tastes, and it shapes this endeavor.

The Division of Humanities and Social Sciences of the California Institute of Technology—the institution where I began my professional life—also fostered interdisciplinary programs. The structure of the department proved most important in 1982, when I returned from Uganda, deeply disturbed, both emotionally and intellectually, by what I had experienced. In search of knowledge of societies similarly scarred by poverty and violence, I turned to the study of European history. The interdisciplinary nature of the institute seamlessly adapted to my needs. Teaching with Philip Hoffman and the late Eleanor Searle, I began to study how peace and order were won from the unpromising materials offered by medieval and early modern Europe. In discussions with colleagues in anthropology Thayer Scudder and Elizabeth Colson, I began to pool the experiences of agrarian and kinship societies today with the experiences of such societies in the past and to apply ideas formulated by students of history to materials compiled by students of contemporary development.

The extraordinary group that assembled at the Center for Advanced Study in the Behavioral Sciences at Stanford in 1993–1994 also shaped this work. Avner Greif, Margaret Levi, Jean-Laurent Rosenthal, and Barry Weingast reinforced my commitment to mixing the study of history with the study of political economy, and particularly the political economy of development.

Thanks too to my students, especially those who have taken Social Analysis 52, a course that I have long offered in Harvard's core curriculum. With a grant from the Ford Foundation, Alison Alter and Smita Singh helped to launch the course. Discussions with my teaching fellows—Mala Htun, Aba Schubert, Melissa Thomas, Anne Wren, James Fowler, and Jeremy Weinstein—deepened my understanding of the issues that it confronted and the materials that it employed.

As important as my experiences in these intellectual communities, however, have been my experiences in the field. Miners in Kitwe, villagers in Luapula, local politicians in Meru, bureaucrats in Uganda, guerrilla fighters in Sudan, diplomats in Bogotá, London, and São Paulo: each has taught me.

This book was written while I was a visiting scholar in the research department of the World Bank. It was revised at the Center for International Development of Harvard University. Special thanks go to Mary Shirley for arranging this appointment at the bank and to Jeffrey Sachs and Sara Sievers for assistance from the center. I also wish to thank Maria Amelina, Macartan Humphreys, Fabrice Lehoucq, Jeffry Frieden, Philil Keefer, Ronald Rogowski, David Laitin, Jean Ensminger, Kenneth Shepsle, Andrei Shleifer, and Andrew Moravcsik for their comments, and to give special thanks to Avner Greif, Peter Hall, Margaret Levi, Jean-Laurent Rosenthal, and Roby Harrington for their close readings of the manuscript. Thanks too to Clark Gibson and Marc Busch for using the manuscript in the classroom, and to their students for comments and suggestions.

While I owe much to my colleagues, my students, and my experiences in the field, to my family, I owe more. I dedicate this book to my in-laws, Helen and the late Joseph Rouse. This book addresses the transition that both triumphantly made from life on the farm to life in the city. It explores the role of the family in facilitating that transition, something that they have recounted with wit, affection, and authority. I owe to both my knowledge of their journey; their parenting of my wife; and their redefinition of the boundaries of their family, as they expanded it to embrace my own.

Cambridge, Massachusetts
21 January 2000

PROSPERITY AND VIOLENCE

1

INTRODUCTION

Time and chance happeneth to them all.

—ECCLESIASTES 9:11

IN A MUSEUM IN NORTH GERMANY, I encountered two cabinets depicting early life in the region. The first contained a model of settlement in the fourth century A.D.; the second a model of the region in the twelfth. Figures 1.1 and 1.2 present the basic outlines.

In the first model, people dwelt in small settlements inland from the sea, seemingly huddled on the sides of a river. They dressed in skins and lived in huts, hunted with spears, and journeyed in boats fabricated from the pelts of animals. Their small settlements appeared fragile, as if designed to facilitate rapid flight from invaders. They resembled uncertain embers in an ocean of darkness: the sea itself, of course, but also the surrounding forest that mounted up from the river, crossed the surrounding hills, and swept east across the continent, giving way to marshes and then to the steppes that led to Asia.

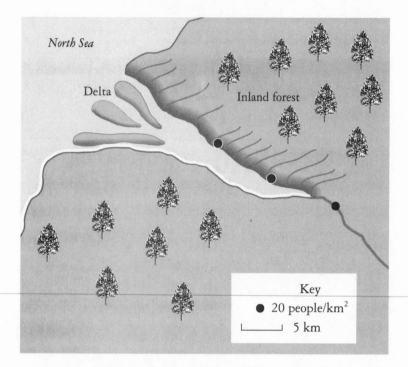

Figure 1.1 North German Settlements circa A.D. 300

As revealed in the second display, centuries later the pattern had changed. Population had grown. Rather than scattered in small camps, most families now lived in dense settlements, surrounded with walls for protection. Settlement had become not only more concentrated, but also, paradoxically, more dispersed. Some families had ventured forth to settle on the shores of the sea. Others had formed camps in the swamplands of the delta and still others had moved inland to dwell in the surrounding forest. By all appearances, most were more prosperous than their ancestors. Their houses were made of timber, not skins; so too their boats. Their clothes were of fiber and their implements artfully crafted. Market stalls stood adjacent to the walls of the settlement, where merchants appeared to exchange the crafts of the

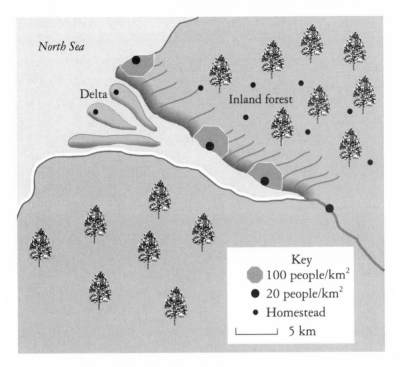

Figure 1.2 North German Settlements circa A.D. 1100

town for fish from the delta, game from the forest, or grain from the surrounding countryside.

The exhibits depicted life in the region centuries before. Exiting the museum, I abruptly reentered the present. The museum stood on a hill overlooking a river, just where it entered the sea. Automobiles sped along the surrounding streets and pedestrians crowded the adjacent sidewalks. Where once there had been a delta, there now lay a harbor, congested by tankers, ferries, and freighters. Across the river, industries lined the embankment, spouting smoke into the basin formed by surrounding hills. The sea beyond the delta lay shrouded by smog from the city.

The story depicted in the museum exhibit captures an oft-told tale. It has been recounted by the archeologists (e.g.,

Carneiro 1970) who reconstruct the past and by social scientists (e.g., Boserup 1981) who study development in modern societies. Karl Polanyi refers to the transition from village to city and from agriculture to industry as "the great transformation" (1944); Kuznets and others refer to it as "structural change" (1966). This book explores the political economy of development by studying the politics and economics of this transformation.

THE FIELD OF DEVELOPMENT

Students of development specialize in the study of the poorer nations of the world. Rather than concentrating on the advanced industrial societies, they focus instead on nations in Asia, Africa, and Latin America that remain heavily rural, largely agricultural, and largely impoverished. The field thus defines itself cross-sectionally, distinguishing rich nations from poor and focusing on the politics of the latter.

While much can and has been learned by proceeding in this fashion, there appears an obvious mismatch between the phenomenon being studied and the data employed. Scholars pursue their research by taking cross sections at one point in time; but development implies the *passage* of time. As approached here, development refers to the growth of per capita incomes and to the transformation of social and political systems. Development, growth, and transformation: each word highlights the temporal, rather than the spatial, element of human societies. The study of development must therefore take into account the passage of time.

My research has focused on contemporary Africa and Latin America and I will repeatedly draw on what I have learned from my work in these regions. But I will also draw upon materials from history. Societies that are now urban, industrial, and wealthy were themselves once rural, agrarian, and poor. I will therefore marshal materials from medieval and early modern Europe. Noting the lessons to be learned from the great power rivalries of the present era—the competition between Communist and capitalist states—I will also seek lessons from the great power rivalries of the past, and in particular that between Britain and France in early modern Europe.

In exploring the historical and contemporary experiences of developing societies, I will address two key themes. One is economic: I will look at ways in which societies increase the average incomes of their members. The other is political: I will explore the institutions they form, the governance structures they create, and, above all, the ways in which they alter—or fail to alter—the use of violence.

CAPITAL

In my discussion of economic development, I will focus on the formation of capital. Capital is the factor of production that spans time. In one period, people may choose to save; withholding resources from present consumption, they may invest them, or form capital. They do so in order to secure the increased possibilities for consumption that investment makes possible. They make present sacrifices in order to secure future gains.

Capital can take the form of a bridge or canal or industrial plant. It can also take the form of a bank account or financial portfolio. But capital need not be physical or monetary. It can also take the form of a skill or a mode of expression, which may itself be costly to acquire. Time that could be spent in pleasure may instead be devoted to study, such that the person can later gain the rewards that accrue to proficiency and attainment.

Classrooms, universities, and apprenticeships: these, as much as banks or industries, constitute loci for the formation of capital.

Because the formation of capital spans time, the decision to invest entails risk. The costs of investment occur in present time; they are therefore certain. The payoffs occur in the future. Future events can therefore render rewards uncertain and alter the incentives to form capital. Fire, flood, or disease can intervene and disrupt the most promising of endeavors. But so too can the conduct of human beings, who may launch wars, overthrow governments, or fail to honor pledges, thus disrupting the plans of others.

In a variety of ways, institutions address the problem of risk. In my analysis of agrarian societies, for example, I shall stress the way in which families provide insurance against costly acts of nature. In such societies, families also provide defenses against the risks arising from the behavior of others; kinship provides a political system, capable of restraining behavior and safeguarding property. As I shall show, kin relations provide insufficient assurances, however, to motivate the formation of the kinds of capital necessary for an industrial society. The assurance kinship provides, moreover, comes at high cost. Analysis of these costs helps us to understand why it is not societies governed by kinship, but rather societies governed by states, that secure the great transformation.

In exploring the political foundations of economic development, I therefore isolate and examine two core, or primitive, actions, one economic and the other political: the decision to form capital and the formation of institutions that render it rational to do so.

ECONOMIC ORGANIZATION

By opening up new lands or purchasing new plant or machinery, or by investing in skills or improvements in the mechanical arts, people can secure higher levels of output per capita and thereby increase the quantity of goods or services they can consume. Economic growth also results from increases in the productivity of land, labor, and capital: by investing in the creation of new technologies, people can increase the level of output they secure from a given quantity of each resource. Equally as important, economic growth results from changes in the manner in which people organize the process of production. In this book, I focus not only on investment but also on organization as a source of economic growth.

The ways in which production is organized affects the level of output. Some kinds of economic activity combine factors of production in ways that simply "scale up," as it were: an increase in the quantity of inputs yields a proportionate increase in the quantity of goods produced. In other kinds of economic activity, however, production is organized in such a manner that an increase in the quantity of inputs yields a more than proportionate increase in output. Output increases as if it were responding not simply to the addition of resources to production but also to the interactions between them. It responds multiplicatively rather than additively to increases in the use of land, labor, and capital.[1]

Agriculture provides an example of the first kind of economic organization. For a given state of the art, when the quantity of land, labor, and capital doubles, then so too does the output from farming. This is not to argue that farming has failed to achieve technological progress, and is thus incapable of growth. With the movement from animal traction to mechani-

---

[1] In this discussion, I omit the distinction between internal and external economies of scale. A more complete analysis would include them, relating one to the creation of markets and towns and the other to the rise of firms. Each serves as sources of growth, but while the first was important in the medieval and early modern period, the latter was important to the era of the Industrial Revolution. Each also gives rise to distinctive political problems, and the argument that I advance can and should be extended to address them.

cal power, with the adoption of new breeds of plant and beast, and with the application of chemical and biological innovations to farming, the output per unit of land and labor has risen dramatically. But economic growth in agriculture has not greatly benefited from changes in economic organization. The form in which agricultural production is organized has altered far less than other aspects of farming. A large corporation may own the farm; the processing of foodstuffs may take place in factories; and the production process may itself be mechanized. But more often than not, the farmer and his household organize the process of production.

If the household is emblematic of the form of organization characteristic of farming, then it is the team that best represents the form employed in industry. Teams allow for forms of production that not only combine inputs into production additively, but that also extract benefits from the members' interaction. In a modern enterprise, one unit of the organization may be in charge of the procurement of raw materials; another of their milling and shaping; and a third of their fabrication into finished products. Other units may provide the services necessary to sustain the production process: the recruitment and training of labor; the purchasing of materials; the financing of the firm; or procurement, sales, and the negotiation of contracts.[2]

In such forms of economic organization, the impact of one unit's effort depends upon the conduct of others. Increases in output result not merely from the sum of the efforts devoted to production, but also from the complementarities among them. Such forms of organization can thus generate increases in output that are more than proportionate to increases in the quanti-

[2] Farmers too perform such tasks. But the seasonal nature of production means that they can be performed sequentially. In industry, they must be performed in parallel.

ties of inputs. The form of organization itself becomes a source of growth.

To illustrate, envisage a firm in a developing society that not only recruits workers but also trains them, teaching them to read, to calculate, and to write. Each unit of the firm gains from the increased supply of educated labor. Not only the plant but also such support services as accounting and sales benefit from the investment. And the productivity of the plant is enhanced by the increased productivity of the staff in these other departments. The complementarities embodied in the structure of the firm thus multiply the impact of the initial investment in training.

All who follow those most visible of teams—those in modern athletics—can quickly grasp that interactions can be productive. But they will also realize that interactions can be perverse. Hazards as well as opportunities result from interdependency within teams. Not only can a member of a team enhance the performance of those about her, she can also sulk, withhold effort, and harm the performance of others. If only for this reason, teams possess managers who can inspire, cajole, or coerce, and so impose discipline. Like sports teams, economic organizations also require governance structures. Firms require managers to coordinate relationships, ensuring that the conduct of one unit of the team enhances, rather than impedes, the performance of others.

The creation of capital provides one source of growth. So too does the formation of economic organizations. And just as the study of the creation of capital leads to the study of politics, so too does the study of organizations. To form economic organizations, those who possess power must delegate it to private hands. They must place it in the hands of those who will govern productive relationships and secure the benefits that can be produced by the complementary efforts of those who employ land, labor, and capital to produce goods and services.

Those who engage in politics, rather than production, specialize in the use of violence. Most commonly, they use power to redistribute, not to create, wealth. As acts of redistribution often inflict losses, the use of force often destroys. For power to be used to produce wealth, coercion must therefore be used in new ways. Those who specialize in the use of force must refrain from violence and delegate their authority to those who will employ it productively. They must delegate it to those who specialize in combining land, labor, and capital in the process of production.

When do kings grant liberties to merchants and burghers? When do political executives vest power and authority in the executives of firms? Why do states, which could easily destroy economic organizations, instead allow them to govern their economies? In exploring the political foundations of economic development, I address these kinds of questions.

In this book I therefore look not only at the manner in which capital is formed. I also look at the way in which violence becomes domesticated, as it were, and is used not to predate or to destroy but rather to strengthen the productive forces of society.

POLITICAL FOUNDATIONS

I had come to northern Germany to interview firms that imported coffee from East Africa. The museum had provided a welcome diversion during a long weekend in which offices were closed and time hung heavy upon me. Leaving the exhibit, I entered a nearby café. The menu offered an inviting selection of hot beverages, including the robusta coffees of Uganda and the mild coffees of Kenya. The warm respite I derived from consuming them could, I knew, be multiplied thousandfold at any instant in northern Europe and a millionfold in any day. Consumers in the developed world sought the products of East Africa and willingly offered a portion of their incomes to procure them.

From my fieldwork in East Africa, I knew that Kenyan merchants, bankers, and industrialists had fashioned a harbor that, while smaller than that of the city in northern Germany, nonetheless resembled it in form and function. To export the coffees of Kenya and Uganda, they had invested in the construction of rail facilities, piers, and warehouses. They had built office buildings and leased out space to brokers, shippers, and insurance firms. They had widened and deepened the harbor, altered the flow of the river, and constructed sidings and terminals. Not only had they thus invested the capital in the perfection of the harbor and the creation of its facilities; but they had also created a governance structure to regulate the flow of traffic from inland, through the port, and thence overseas. By act of the Kenyan Parliament, they had formed a corporation that vested the management of the port in an executive who could hire and fire managers and deputies and who possessed the power to order, to discipline, and to fine, and thus to govern the flow of goods through the facility.

In response to the economic opportunities offered by the demand for tropical products in the Northern Hemisphere, then, investors had created in East Africa a productive economic organization and the state had delegated to its management the power to govern its activities. There coffee was bulked and crated by blue-collar workers; inspected and insured by clerks; and shipped in containers, lifted by cranes onto ships made of steel. On the coast of East Africa, the demand for coffee had evoked the creation of an industrial form of economic activity.

As my research took me inland, I learned that not only capitalists but also peasants had responded to the demands of consumers in the industrialized nations. For several months, I worked in Meru, a district that lies on the slopes of Mount Kenya. Coffee production had rendered the district prosperous, and small towns dotted the mountainside, containing shops owned by artisans who produced clothing, footwear, furniture, and farm implements. Churches, banks, bars, restaurants, and hotels lined the streets. On weekends, farmers and their families gathered in town, some entering on foot, others emerging from crowded taxis, and a fortunate few descending from their own vehicles.

Farmers in Meru had prospered from the production of coffee. With the proceeds they had earned, some had invested in cattle. Many had financed the education of their children, some of whom attended elementary school in the village, others secondary school in town, and some universities abroad. Many of those who secured an education had then taken jobs in the cities; maintaining ties with their families at home, they funneled a portion of their earnings back to the farms and shops of Meru. Even during a drought in 1985—the year I worked in the district—Meru, its farmers, and its towns radiated a sheen of prosperity and well-being that reflected the successful response of its peasants to the opportunities provided by exports of coffee.

Departing the farms at the foot of Mount Kenya, I then journeyed farther inland and crossed into Bugisu, a coffee-producing region lying on the slopes of Mount Elgon in Uganda. There too farmers had invested in the production of coffee, and towns had sprung up to provide them the means to ship their crop, to collect payment, and to make purchases for their farms and families. But prosperity and tranquility, I soon learned, lay in Bugisu's past; stagnation and fear characterized its present.

Unlike the streets of the towns in Meru, those in Bugisu were not crowded with farmers hurriedly making purchases or leisurely enjoying the pleasure of town; rather, they were occupied by soldiers, while farmers fearfully huddled on their homesteads in the forests. Youths did not stroll about in school uniforms, as they had in Meru; in Bugisu, they instead marched, lockstep, in military garb, lashed by the voices—and the belts—of their commanders. On the farms, the coffee-bearing trees remained unpruned; diseases ran unchecked from plant to plant and farm to farm; and stocks accumulated, for want of the ability of merchants to finance the purchase of the crop or its transport to the coast.

By venturing from the coast inland, I was therefore forcefully introduced to the link between prosperity and violence. In the coastal harbor, force was not absent; rather, it was structured and organized. In Meru, prosperity was undergirded by peace. In Uganda, the fear spread by violence undermined the willingness to invest or to engage in economic activity. Such comparisons and contrasts highlight the significance of the political foundations for development.

Development involves the formation of capital and the organization of economic activity. Politically, it involves the taming of violence and the delegation of authority to those who will use power productively. Just as this introduction has cut from Europe to Africa to make these points, so too will the text move from materials from history to those drawn from modern societies in an effort to explore these themes.

2

AGRARIAN
SOCIETIES

*Every family naturally tended to become larger and the head of
every family wanted to grow richer, so that he could . . . increase
the numbers of men and women . . . in his household.*
> —GEORGES DUBY, *FRANCE IN THE*
> *MIDDLE AGES, 987–1460,* XI

SOCIETIES THAT ARE NOW urban and industrial were once
rural and agrarian. Prior to the great transformation, the lives of
their people resembled the lives of those who now dwell in what
we call developing societies. They lived in homesteads and
hamlets, supported themselves by farming, and organized production, social life, and the affairs of their communities through
the medium of their families.

In agrarian societies, families organize production, consumption, and the accumulation of wealth, be it monetary or in the
form of cattle, land, or dependents. They also manage the use of
power. Not only daily life but also affairs of state flow through the

networks spun by birth, marriage, and descent. For better or worse, the actions of the Habsburgs, the Romanovs, the Tudors, and the Bourbons dictated much of the history of what are now the advanced industrial nations of Europe. And the House of Saud in Arabia, the al-Tikriti clan in Iraq, the Gandhis in India, the Bhuttos in Pakistan, the Zias in Bangladesh, or the "dynastic families" (Paige 1997) in Central America—the Ariases, Cristianis, Chamorros, and others—shape the course of politics in today's developing nations.

Societies dominated by kinship are often seen as static. Political sociologists, such as Weber, view them as preoccupied with the "eternal yesterday" (1958, 78) and therefore as tradition-bound and unchanging. Anthropologists often cast them in the "timeless present," describing the lives of their members as if they were suspended in amber. And while conceding the efficiency of their practices, neoclassical economists nonetheless stress the poverty of such societies, which results, they claim, from their failure to invest in technical change (e.g., Schultz 1976). Unwittingly forging a consensus that spans the ideological divide of our times, Marxist anthropologists (e.g., Meillassoux 1981, Godelier 1972) join in this characterization, consigning kinship societies to the category of "pre-capitalist." Their members may occupy land; through kinship, they may organize and control labor, and thereby engage in exploitation; but they lack capital, and therefore can merely replicate, rather than transform, themselves.

The argument of this chapter is that this consensus is wrong. If only as a consequence of demographic change, such societies are dynamic; they expand, differentiate, and engage in exchange and conflict. Pace Weber, in the presence of change and differentiation, their members employ reason and make choices; pace the Marxist anthropologists and neoclassical economists, they form capital, albeit in the context of kinship rather than markets.

This point was forcefully taught to me by an old man in the copper belt of Zambia. Although among the last regions of Africa to be occupied by the British, the copper belt soon became one of the most industrialized; within fifty years of its occupation, a score of mining towns rendered it among the most urbanized as well. As astronomers use the light cast by receding stars to study the origins of the universe, so too do social scientists study the life of the Zambian copper belt to comprehend the formation of modern societies. As a graduate student, I journeyed there to probe the process by which industries grow, cities form, and labor forces assemble. "Look behind you," the old man said: "See that smelter?" Pausing for effect, he then announced: "I built it." His employment records confirmed that he had indeed been employed in its construction. From him I then learned of how his family, hearing of new jobs to be had in the town, had given him food and *indalama* (money) for his journey; how, having secured a job, he had sent back first for his younger brothers and then for his nephews; how, while in town, he had sent money to his mother and uncles and visited his village to take part in weddings and funerals; and how, as his retirement drew near, he then sent money home to purchase cattle and build a toolshed and a *duka* (country store) on land set aside for him by the village headman, into whose family his sister had married.

This man's family had invested in his migration to town. He had helped to build the plant that refined a major portion of the ores mined in Zambia. He in turn invested the money he had earned in town in his family and his village. Through his life, the aged miner had demonstrated how persons in agrarian societies probe for opportunities and, drawing on the resources of kin, form capital.

Building on the insights offered by the wizened miner from

the copper belt, this chapter explores the economic role of families in developing societies. It also evaluates the quality of the protection that they provide against damaging acts of nature and human beings. While stressing on the one hand the economic vitality and political capabilities of kinship societies, on the other it stresses that their political institutions constrain what their economies can achieve. Confined by the institutions that structure their lives, members of lineage societies confront a trade-off between prosperity and peace—a trade-off they later escape as part of the great transformation.

THE ECONOMICS OF KINSHIP

In addressing the economics of lineage societies, we may best start with an example. Of the many from which to choose, I select the Kikuyu, a society in central Kenya. As I shall several times return to this example, I provide (Figure 2.1) a cross section of a portion of the highlands wherein they dwell.

The mountains of central Kenya, with their rich volcanic soils, temperate climate, and abundant and reliable rainfall, offer the Kikuyu a highly favorable location for agriculture. Growing beans, vegetables, maize, and fruit, and raising livestock, the Kikuyu have prospered and multiplied and their homesteads have spread into the lower elevations. Livestock use more land than do gardens; and as the highlands became crowded, families dispatched their goats and cattle to the lowlands. Releasing lands from pastoral use, the Kikuyu thereby freed up space for gardens in the core. As the younger members of the family herded cattle on the periphery, they marked out sites for new homesteads. Where they made contact with other peoples, they negotiated rights of passage for their herds and

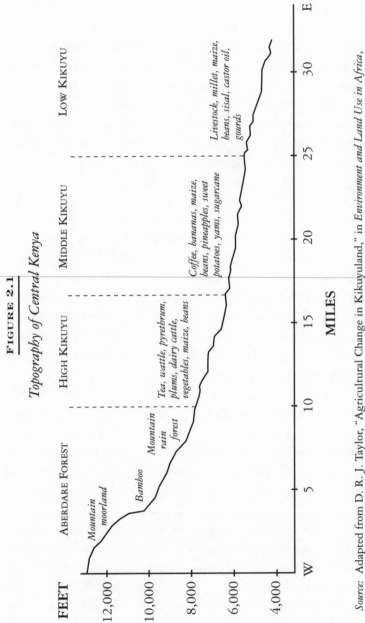

FIGURE 2.1

Topography of Central Kenya

FEET

12,000

10,000

8,000

6,000

4,000

W · 5 · 10 · 15 · 20 · 25 · 30 · E

MILES

ABERDARE FOREST — HIGH KIKUYU — MIDDLE KIKUYU — LOW KIKUYU

Mountain moorland

Bamboo

Mountain rain forest

Tea, wattle, pyrethrum, plums, dairy cattle, vegetables, maize, beans

Coffee, bananas, maize, beans, pineapples, sweet potatoes, yams, sugarcane

Livestock, millet, maize, beans, sisal, castor oil, gourds

Source: Adapted from D. R. J. Taylor, "Agricultural Change in Kikuyuland," in *Environment and Land Use in Africa,* eds. M. F. Thomas and G. W. Whittington (London: Methuen, 1959), p. 485.

rights of occupation for new settlements—rights they hoped, by guile or force of numbers, to turn into rights of ownership. Expansion, infiltration, settlement, and the dispatching of younger households to the periphery—this dynamic marks the history of this people and its constituent kinship units. The story of the Kikuyu is paralleled in Africa by the story of the Mossi, the Ashanti, the Nuer, the Tswana, and the Tiv.[1] In Latin America it finds its parallel in the history of settlement in Antioquia in central Colombia (Parsons 1949); in North America, in the spread of settlers through the Ohio Valley and into the Western Plains; in Asia, in the expansion of Russian peoples to the south and west (Blum 1961); and in Europe, by the sweep of the Germanic tribes west and south into the territories claimed by Rome (Ausenda 1995; Bartlett 1993).

The history of agrarian societies, such as the Kikuyu, can be addressed as a series of themes. Taken together, they offer insight into the origins of, and limits to, prosperity in kinship societies.

MIGRATION

The first families to arrive in a region naturally tend to settle in the ecologically most favored locations. While rainfall may be sparse, seasonal, or erratic in the lowlands, the mountains often receive high levels of moisture the year round, and at regular intervals. While temperatures may vary dramatically in the lowlands, they remain relatively stable and temperate in the moisture-laden atmosphere of the higher elevations, providing a favorable climate for agriculture. At times of peril, moreover,

---

[1] See, for example, Leakey (1977); Evans-Pritchard (1940); Bohannan (1989); Werbner (1993); and Saul (1993).

the inhabitants can take refuge in upland redoubts, and thereby protect themselves from aggressors. As was the case of the Kikuyu, migrants may therefore settle first in the rich volcanic soils of the highlands.

Seeking to farm well and safely, families therefore settle in favored locations. With the passage of time, as new households form, population increases and, with it, the density of settlement. To increase their food supplies, families may press into service the elderly or very young. Alternatively, they may bring into production less fertile lands: those that lie on thin or rocky soils, or those that lie in more remote or forested locations and therefore require greater inputs of labor. Because of the use of either less productive labor or more marginal land, the increase in population is not matched by comparable increases in output. The average level of consumption therefore declines.

In response to diminishing returns in the core, population begins to spread to the periphery. Families begin to search for new farm sites. Staking a younger member to food and funds for his journey, inhabitants of the old settlement dispatch the cadet as if he were a scout, sending him out to explore the periphery. Once the junior locates a favorable locale, his kin soon follow. As families grow, they therefore expand both in number and extent, ramifying through diverse ecologies and infiltrating new territories. Families thereby acquire new resources. The investment in the initial costs of migration yields a subsequent return.

The family thus functions both as an instrument of territorial expansion (Sahlins 1961) and of investment. Even in precapitalist societies, people form capital.

MARKETS

The process of migration generates a dispersion of population. As a consequence, families come to occupy a diverse set of ecological niches. They therefore gain the opportunity to specialize in production and to engage in exchange; that is, they form markets and thereby increase their welfare. By doing so, they not only increase their expected incomes but also reduce the level of the risks they confront in rural life.

Returning to Figure 2.1, we see that the East African highlands constitute a diverse terrain with opportunities for specialization and trade. The higher elevations yield timber and bamboo from the forests and vegetables from the clearings. As the elevation declines and the forest becomes less dense, people shift into the production of maize, potatoes, and beans. The duration of the growing period diminishes as the altitude declines, and at lower altitudes the production of maize therefore gives way to the production of millet and sorghum, which ripen more quickly. At still lower elevations, precipitation becomes uncertain and standing crops therefore give way to grazing livestock that can be herded to where rain has recently fallen. Homesteads along the lakes in the valley below provide base camps for the cattle herders, places to plant gardens, and opportunities for fishing.

The diversity of the ecosystem thus promotes diversity in production and, with it, exchange over space. Traders move up the hills, bringing fish, meat, and leather; they return down, bearing timber and vegetables and medicines gathered in the forests. The diversity also promotes exchange over time. As the rains abate, the growing season ends and the harvest begins. Typically the end of the growing season arrives first at the lower elevations; the harvest then moves upward from the lowlands to the plateau and foothills and then up the sides of the mountains. At the end of the harvest, families possess more food than they can consume; many therefore sell a portion of their crop to others who have not yet harvested, only to purchase foodstuffs later in the year as they await the ripening of their crops.

In this diversified ecological setting, then, markets dot the mountainside or stand at crossroads in the flatlands below. Each exhibits a wide range of products, each produced in its own special habitat. The dispersion of settlement down the mountainside and into the foothills, plateaus, and lowlands thus results in specialization and trade.

RISK

Agrarian societies are societies at risk. Drought, disease, erosion, flood; too little water, or too much—these acts of nature directly impact upon the welfare of rural societies. Nature can be bounteous, but it also can be cruel.

Industrial societies possess markets for risk. People can purchase insurance, thereby protecting themselves against misfortune. Through financial markets, they can borrow in times of need. But pre-industrial societies lack such opportunities. People in such societies cannot shed risk by transacting in markets. Instead, they must directly bear the costs of uncertainty; they must self-insure. Two of the most obvious ways in which they do so is by making "conservative" decisions and by "failing" to specialize.

Technocrats often bewail the reluctance of peasant farmers to grow crops that yield demonstrably greater yields than do those that they traditionally cultivate. But like most people, farmers are risk averse. In comparing two streams of income, they therefore evaluate not only their average but also their variability; it is the latter that suggests the likelihood of a bad outcome. They accept a lower expected yield as the price they must pay for a lower variance. As a result, they make "conservative" decisions: they grow crops that while offering a smaller harvest nonetheless offer one that is more certain.

Farmers also diversify. Rather than specializing in the production of maize or wheat or rice, many instead grow a full array of crops; in other words, they grow "food." Should birds descend upon the millet crop, the gourds and vegetables at least might be spared. Farmers thus often remain subsistence producers. They are reluctant to plant pure stands of maize or wheat or to specialize in the production of cash crops. Uncertainty thus limits the degree to which they specialize. In a world pervaded by risk and devoid of means for shedding it, the necessity for self-insurance induces caution.

Both conservatism and the failure to specialize impose costs. A farmer who clings to a practice that is tried and true will fail to secure the benefits of technical change. The farmer who grows "food" will fail to secure the profits to be made by devoting his resources to the production of a crop that he could then profitably exchange for others. The costs in terms of the diminution of income yield, however, the benefit of increased security. It secures the peace of mind that comes from decreased risk in the face of hostile nature.

People in agrarian societies possess another form of insurance: their families. Return to Figure 2.1 and recall the attendant discussion. Those who lived at different elevations dwelt in different ecosystems, with different endowments of land, moisture, temperature, and sunshine. As a result of living in different ecosystems, they produced different crops. More to the point, they also faced different kinds of risks.

It is useful to think of a farm as an asset. Like any asset, a farm yields a stream of income that possesses an expected return that is uncertain. The mean provides a measure of the expected value of that return; the variance, a measure of its uncertainty. Farm sites located at different points in the topography—one high up the mountain, another in the coffee zone, a third on the plains below, as depicted in Figure 2.1—can therefore be thought of as yielding streams of income, each with its own mean and variance.

In such a setting, it makes sense to retain large families. For the mathematics of chance tells us that the expected value of the combination of two independent assets is the sum of their means. But it also tells that the variance of the combination of two independent assets may be *less* than the sum of their variances.[2]

Consider a household dwelling on the plains for example. By the rules of the lineage, this household would possess a right to share in the earnings of other households in the kin group, including those dwelling higher up the mountain. Given the diversity of the environment, a bad year for the household in the plains might correspond to a normal one at the higher elevation. And given the norm of kinship property, a family subject to drought in the plains possesses the right to take refuge with more fortunately situated kin. Family members can exercise the right to a share of the property of other relatives to insure themselves against risk. By extension, all members of the kin group likewise benefit from this source of insurance. Each ecological niche may be subject to random shocks; but by dwelling in kin groups that span diverse locations, people reduce their exposure to risk.

Membership in families is costly. If living in a low elevation, a household can expect to have to support relatives from

---

[2] Consider the value of two assets, x and y, each of which is randomly distributed with variances Var (x) and Var (y). By distributing his holdings equally among the two, an economic agent could secure a stream of income whose variance would be:

$$\text{Var} \left(\tfrac{1}{2}x + \tfrac{1}{2}y \right) = \tfrac{1}{4}\text{Var}\,(x) + \tfrac{1}{4}\text{Var}\,(y) + 2\,\text{Cov}\,(xy).$$

Because the variance of the value of each is reduced by $\tfrac{1}{4}$, and because the covariance can be negative, the diversification of holdings reduces risk.

the high zones when conditions there turn bad. But such costs constitute the price of insurance. Acknowledging the rights of family members to a share of the income generated by "its" farm entitles the household to live off the proceeds of highland brethren when misfortune strikes. That property rights inhere in families, rather than in individuals, renders families a means of insurance.

In an earlier section, I argued that families provide means for investing; costs devoted to migration reduce the impact of diminishing returns in the core and yield control over assets in the periphery. In this section, I argue that expansion not only yields higher incomes; insofar as it entails dispersion, it yields incomes that are more certain as well. The dispersed location of the family estate yields a diversified portfolio of income-generating assets, thus reducing the level of risk.[3]

RURAL SOCIETIES ARE DYNAMIC. As population increases over time, families disperse and ramify. Rural societies form capital. Elders sponsor the emigration of younger kin and, in so doing, increase the welfare of the family and its claim over resources. Through migration and settlement, agrarian societies promote the formation of markets and put in place means not only for raising the expected level of their incomes but also for lowering their risks.

Rural societies thus devise means for enhancing their welfare. And yet, as already seen, they confront limitations in their

---

[3] It is notable that in the East African highlands, lineages and ethnic groups run vertically up and down the mountain in strips, rather than girding the mountain in rings. By doing so, they decrease the covariance among the ecological niches that they occupy.

ability to do so. In the absence of technological change, diminishing returns reduces the per capita level of income; as people crowd upon the land, the average income declines. Conservatism ties people to the use of low-yielding crops. And self-insurance offers an expensive form of risk bearing; limiting specialization reduces the benefits to be gained from market exchange. The arrangements that agrarian societies forge, while admirable, thus constrain the wealth they can generate.

Just as families and kin groups self-insure against the risks of nature, so too do they self-insure against risks arising from the conduct of other human beings. Further constraining the economic performance of kinship societies is the nature of their political institutions. While offering a means for protecting property, the private provision of security by family and kin, I argue, also limits the accumulation of wealth.

THE POLITICS OF KINSHIP

Just as acts of nature impose risks upon people, so too do the actions of human beings. Sahlins stresses that in agrarian societies, economic relations are not just related to social arrangements but rather "embedded" in them (1971, 8). So too are political relations, as people seek to render their families sources of security and instruments of protection in the face of threats by others.

In such societies, coercion is often privately supplied. People not only produce and consume. They also fight. Among the arts they practice are the arts of war.

Some fight in order to increase their wealth. History is filled with legends of conquest, as bands of warriors set out in search of plunder. Others devote resources to the defense of their possessions. Whether by building walls, digging moats, or with-drawing into remote locations, or whether by training in com-bat, honing skills and weapons, or cultivating a fearsome reputation, people seek to deter others from encroaching upon their persons or their property. The need for such defenses increases with the value of their possessions. The more numerous and precious their belongings, the greater the incentive to steal and the greater therefore the need to organize protection.

The migration of people, the accumulation of assets, and the growth of trade: as each then contributes to the growth of income, each also increases the temptation to engage in preda-tion—and the value of deterring it.

AN EXAMPLE: THE NUER

Evans-Pritchard, a noted anthropologist who worked among the Nuer of southern Sudan, sought to explain how a society based purely on kinship—i.e., one lacking a bureaucracy, a court system, or police—nonetheless curtailed theft and defended rights in property (1940). Among the answers he gave was one based upon what he called "segmentary opposition"; phrased differently, the answer lay in the threat of retaliation by others, or the feud.[4]

The Nuer are a pastoralist people. While they do cultivate gardens, they engage principally in herding. As Evans-Pritchard puts it, the Nuer "not only depend on cattle for many of life's necessities but they have the herdsman's outlook on the world. Cattle are their dearest possession" (1940, 16). Cattle provide the principal store of wealth for the Nuer, he writes, and the joint family—the father, his sons, and their wives—constitutes the ele-

---

[4] The following section draws heavily on chapter 1 of Bates (1983).

mentary property-holding unit. Each family seeks to care for and increase its cattle holdings.

Among the Nuer, breeding and raising cattle provides one path to prosperity. Theft offers another. Each property owner could make himself better off by stealing the cattle of others. And every indication is that the Nuer are tempted to do so. They certainly raid the cattle holdings of neighboring tribes; thus, Evans-Pritchard writes, the Nuer "gladly risk their lives to . . . pillage [the cattle of] their neighbors" (1940, 16). The strength of their desire to steal is suggested by Evans-Pritchard when he recounts: "As my Nuer servant once said to me: 'You can trust a Nuer with any amount of money, pounds and pounds and pounds, and go away for years and return and he will not have stolen it; but a single cow—that is a different matter" (1940, 49).

The puzzle, from Evans-Pritchard's point of view, was that despite the potential for theft and disorder the Nuer in fact tended to live in relative harmony. Insofar as the Nuer raided cattle, they tended to raid the cattle of others; raids within the tribe were rare. Somehow the Nuer appear to have avoided the potentially harmful effects arising from greed and self-interest. And they appear to have done so even while lacking those formal institutions so common to Western societies: the courts, the police, and the other appurtenances of the state. Evans-Pritchard devoted much of his efforts to determining how the Nuer, in the absence of such institutions, nonetheless achieved order in their society.

Among the several explanations he advanced, one stands out: the importance of deterrence. Nuer society, he stressed, contains a multitude of internal cleavages. Within villages, families stand in opposition to one another; in conflicts within the larger ward, families in one village align in opposition to the members of another; and within the tribe, the power of one lineage checks that of another. The wrongs that one unit might threaten therefore confront the possibility of retaliation by another.

By Evans-Pritchard's account, the Nuer appreciate the role of deterrence and know that they must unambiguously and forcefully communicate their willingness to retaliate in order to prevent predation. As he states: "It is the knowledge that a Nuer is brave and will stand up against aggression and enforce his property rights by club and spear that ensures respect for person and property" (1940, 171). He further emphasizes the point when he distinguishes between zones of peace and violence in Nuer society. It is precisely in those zones in which a man can recruit kin to engage in battle and thus credibly threaten reprisal, he contends, that disputes are most likely to be settled peacefully (1940, 150ff). The very readiness of the Nuer to employ violence provides a reason, then, that violence so rarely takes place.

Evans-Pritchard's account of the Nuer offers, in the words of Max Gluckman (1955), an account of "peace within the feud." Societies that rely upon households to enforce property rights are societies in which peace is secured by the fear of retaliation. As Evans-Pritchard's account makes clear, such a system *can* work; after all, by his account, the Nuer did live peacefully, in spite of the temptation of theft. But what Evans-Pritchard fails to make clear are the high costs of this political system—costs that include the poverty of Nuer society.

THE LIMITS OF KINSHIP

For deterrence to work, the threat of revenge must be credible. This system of governance requires, then, that men be warriors, capable of inflicting harm; it also requires that they be willing to retaliate, and be known to be willing to do so.

In exploring the wellsprings of credibility, students of kinship societies stress the role of beliefs. Some recount the conviction that those who die with anger in their hearts wander, like Hamlet's ghost, between heaven and earth, demanding revenge (Hardy, 1963). Others stress beliefs in witchcraft, noting that unpropitiated wrongs result in pain, illness, and misfortune among those who inflicted them, or among those who failed to punish transgressors. Such beliefs harden the hearts and steel the hands of those who might otherwise be reluctant to seek revenge. Other scholars stress the role of values, and especially the importance of honor. Knowing that another is honor-bound to seek revenge, they stress, a potential wrongdoer might pause to recalculate the benefits of transgressing. In societies where families arm themselves and provide their own protection, military prowess lies embedded in codes of honor, from which it derives credibility as a deterrent.

When the threat of retaliation works, the private provision of coercion can produce peace, as Evans-Pritchard argued; but the behaviors and beliefs that supply peace also encourage behavior that increases the likelihood of violence. In such societies, private warriors populate public places; people bearing arms and intimating their willingness to employ them strut in the boulevards and cluster in the marketplace. Public places are populated with *provocateurs*; where families are honor-bound to protect their own, hot-tempered youths find protection against the consequences of brazen behavior. Interactions thus take place in a volatile ambience of honor and impudence; young hotheads move to the fore; and a culture of machismo permeates the society. The private provision of security thus creates a hair-trigger society. Provocative acts become commonplace—but also uncommonly dangerous because they can unleash violent reprisals.

The private provision of security is thus fragile. Moreover, it is unforgiving. When retaliation takes place, then honor requires that the punishment itself be revenged. Absent a reputation for being willing to fight, a person becomes vulnerable. Not only might his enemies view him as easy prey, but also his family and friends will scorn him, since their safety depends upon the support that can be expected from others. The incentives to fight thus run deep and once concord is lost, cycles of retaliation ensue.

Private violence *can* work; it can produce peace. But the peace it produces is fragile. Once triggered, the system inflicts costs that mount over time: families span generations, and the wrongs of one generation cast a curse on the lives of those who succeed them. Thus it is that the ancients wrote their history in terms of conflict among families, and in so doing shaped our notion of tragedy. Even after the passage of centuries, the destruction of the House of Atreus evokes feelings of pity and fear. And the fate of Romeo and Juliet, victims of a feud between two families, still kindles our tears.

To avoid the costs of private violence, people seek ways of insuring that retaliation will not be triggered. In so doing, they expose another defect of the private provision of security: in the face of the costs of the system, people may seek to increase their welfare by choosing to live in poverty. Students of village societies emphasize the fear of envy. Others describe how those who become wealthy are subject to accusations of witchcraft and sorcery. In such societies, egalitarianism becomes a strategy in which persons forgo consumption for the sake of peaceful relations with neighbors. To forestall predation, they may simply choose to live without goods worth stealing. In such a setting, poverty becomes the price of peace.

As kinship societies expand, families inhabit diverse terrains; they trade and, better insured against the risks of nature, they secure economic gains. But the nature of their political institutions imposes important limitations upon their well-being. The security they supply to the producers and accumulators of wealth is fragile. It lies imbedded in a culture of provocation. And should threats that support the peace have to be acted upon, then the system produces desolation and grief. The political institutions of kinship societies impose a cruel trade-off: peace on the one hand and prosperity on the other.

During my stay in Uganda, I ventured far beyond the confines of Bugisu. As did many others, I joined teams of specialists who sought to aid in the reconstruction of the country, which was just beginning to recover from the devastation inflicted by the tyrant Idi Amin. On long car rides during the day, or while sharing drinks at night, I came to know several of my counterparts well. And they helped me to understand what it is like to live in a world engulfed by violence. For them, the overthrow of Idi Amin had brought an end to their professional isolation; no longer a pariah state, Uganda could now send its technocrats abroad for conferences and training. But rather than feeling exhilarated, they felt depressed. In the war that led to his overthrow, villages and communities had secured weapons; once armed, people began to pillage the property of their enemies and to punish those who had once pillaged them. Within the districts, villages, and neighborhoods where my colleagues resided, friends and family were now caught up in cycles of violence and retribution. Given the circumstances under which they lived, what joy could they take in their new opportunities? What sense did it make to invest in further training? Too often they came to the office to find a co-worker missing or attending the funeral of a friend.

As we got to know one another, our discussion moved from our professions to our families and loved ones. I then learned of a central question that they confronted: In the midst of violence, how should they best raise their children? How do you teach a child to work hard, to go to school, or to be honest, when that child may die young? And why should a child, or anyone else, do without today, when there may not be a tomorrow?

Members of agrarian societies can and do seek to invest. As in the process of migration, by sacrificing today, they seek to secure future benefits. In such societies, however, the pursuit of improvement is checked. As noted by my Ugandan counterparts, when the future is uncertain, investment, though desirable, may not be a rational act. For the private provision of coercion provides security only within the penumbra of violence.

In the next chapter, I turn to the transformation of the use of force. In so doing, I seek to detect the political forces that break the fetters limiting the development of agrarian societies.

3

THE FORMATION OF
STATES

*A monarch is like "a robber permanently on the prowl, always
probing, . . . always searching for . . . something . . . to steal."*
—THIRTEENTH-CENTURY ENGLISH CHRONICLER,
QUOTED IN RALPH V. TURNER,
KING JOHN, 3

COERCION AND FORCE are as much a part of everyday life as
are markets and economic exchange. In the process of development, however, coercion alters in nature. Rather than being
privately provided, it instead becomes publicly provisioned.
And rather than providing a means for engaging in costly acts
of redistribution, it becomes a means for promoting the creation of wealth.

Drawing from materials on European history, this chapter
traces the change from rural societies, based on agriculture and
farming, to urban societies, based on commerce and manufacturing. It also traces the change from the private provision of

violence, based upon kin and community, to the public provision of coercion, based upon the monarchy and the state. These economic and political transformations, I argue, are intimately related. The rise of towns produced an increase in incomes and the new wealth incited increased conflict. Specialists in the use of violence needed revenues to fight their wars; and those who prevailed were those who allied their political force with the economic fortunes of the towns. The result of this alliance was a new political and economic order—one based on capital and complex economic organizations, one in which prosperity profitably coexisted with peace, and one in which coercion was used not for predation but rather to enhance the productive use of society's resources.

WEALTH AND VIOLENCE

During the fourteenth and fifteenth centuries, the locus of economic growth in Europe shifted from the Mediterranean city-states of Italy to the shores of the Baltic and North Seas. The discovery of the so-called New World and the growth of the Atlantic trade accelerated this transformation and rendered it a permanent feature of Europe's economic geography. The rise of new cities both marked and promoted the rise of prosperity; it brought economic growth not only to the urban areas but also to the north European countryside. In accordance with the logic of the previous chapter, the rise in prosperity brought as well an increase in political violence. Limitations in the quality of political order supplied by the private provision of protection created a demand for a better system of providing it. And specialists in violence who tapped into the wealth of the cities secured the resources to provide that order.

THE RISE OF TOWNS

The Rhine and its tributaries drain a major portion of the interior of northwestern Europe; so do the Schelde and the Somme. Sweeping soils down from the highlands, the rivers built up the rich plateaus and lowlands that stand close to the sea. In Flanders, the Brabant, and the regions now united into the Netherlands, towns formed near the point where each entered the ocean, helping to organize exchange between the populations that clustered along each river's banks with those who dwelt along the banks of others. By the fifteenth century, several of these cities—e.g., Bruges, Ghent, and Antwerp—numbered among Europe's largest. Because of the close links that it maintained with these towns, London too formed an integral part of this rapidly growing region.

The rise of urban centers closely intertwined with the rise of rural prosperity. By river and road, goods entered the cities from the countryside. In warehouses and on docks, wholesalers broke shipments into lots and consigned them to retailers, who reloaded them onto boat, barge, or wagon. The goods then disappeared back into the rural areas, where the majority of the consumers resided. As markets expanded, goods originated from more distant locations; it was often the burghers who provided the transport services, be it by wagon along the roadways, by barge along the rivers, or by boat across the seas. With the growth of trade, exchanges began to take place not only over greater distances but also over longer periods of time. And the burghers then added the provision of credit and the clearance of payments to the services they provided rural dwellers.

As the population of the urban centers rose, so too did the demand for agricultural products. The residents of the cities consumed but did not produce food. To secure food, the urban population therefore had to trade for it, thus strengthening the role of markets in rural society. The growth of cities therefore fostered the commercialization of agriculture.

The value of land and the cost of transport shaped the response of farmers. Near town, land was expensive; urban dwellers competed with farmers for it, thus increasing its value. Farmers in peri-urban districts therefore specialized in the production of vegetables, pigs, and poultry, each of which made efficient use of land. They also produced dairy products that, being bulky, were expensive to transport or could quickly spoil and therefore were best produced close to the point of consumption. Farther from the city, farmers engaged in activities such as cattle raising that made more intensive use of the land or produced goods with high value-to-weight ratios, capable of withstanding high costs of transport.

The commercialization of agriculture stimulated not only the provision of services from urban dwellers, but also infusions of capital. In the delta regions, investors financed the clearing of the land, the draining of swamps, and the transformation of silt into gardens and pastures. Engineering control over the level and flow of water and augmenting the quantity and quality of the land, they rendered the lowlands centers of both commerce and farming.

THE RISE OF VIOLENCE

With an increase in the profits from agriculture, families began to invest in and to improve their farms. To enhance the productivity of their holdings, they added to their household specialists in farming and others who provided skills in writing, in calculating, in breeding and training livestock, in managing laborers and tenants, or in forging implements. These additions to their households also provided muscle and brawn, enabling the landowners to enhance the security of their holdings. The retainers served in indenture, laying claim to a lifelong stream of benefits—food and shelter, in the household of their employer—in exchange for their services and for the obligation, when called upon, to fight.

Family ties yield means for coping with risks arising from acts of nature. The accumulation of retainers provided a means for coping with risks arising from the actions of men. Working in the fields or at their trades or when idle, these employees could rapidly be mobilized for conflict. The provision of livings and the accommodation of muscular hangers-on assured a subsequent flood of men into the field of battle, should anyone threaten the owner's rights in property. The growth of the economy of northwestern Europe was thus accompanied by the militarization of households.

The private provision of violence was costly. Only those who stood to lose much possessed an incentive to provide it. In practice, this meant that the political and economic elite became one in the rural areas, with households that were rich also becoming the households that dominated militarily the hinterlands of northwestern Europe.

It is notable that the locus of rural violence concentrated in the areas most deeply integrated with the new urban economies. Hechter and Brustein (1980, 1081) have provided a map of "peasant rebellions" in the fifteenth century; such conflicts were often led by elites, who mobilized kin and dependents to fight. Hechter and Brustein's map (Figure 3.1), suggests that the spatial distribution of rural conflict corresponded closely to that of commercial agriculture.

In their interpretation of their findings, Hechter and Brustein (1980) note further that it was in such areas that "feudalism" had emerged, as well as economic growth. The interpretation I provide suggests why economic growth, violence, and

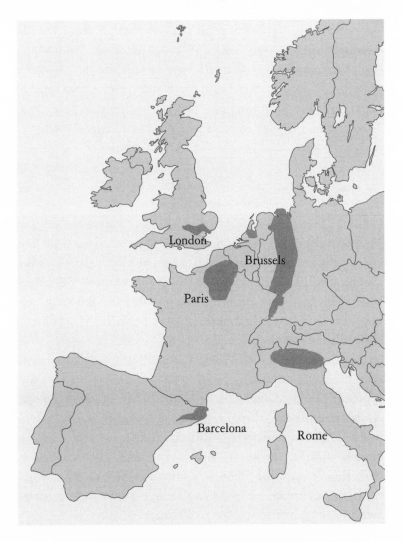

Figure 3.1 Principal Areas of Rural Conflict in
Fourteenth-Century Western Europe

Source: Adapted from Michael Hechter and Willam Brustein, 1980, "Regional
Modes of Production and Patterns of State Formation in Western Europe,"
American Journal of Sociology 85, no. 5, p. 1081. Copyright 1980 by the
University of Chicago. Reprinted with permission

the rise of feudal political organization would go together. By creating wealth, growth elicits violence; and it was landowning elites who had the incentive privately to organize the defense of property. Feudalism was based upon the private provision of coercion; it involved the militarization of the rural household. That it should emerge in zones of growing prosperity was therefore to be expected, given the logic of this argument.

TAMING VIOLENCE

Prosperity spread inland along the river systems, up the Rhine and southward into France, and across the Channel to incorporate London, East Anglia, and the southern counties of England. But along with that prosperity came violence, privately provided by elite kin groups and households, with the support of their liveried retainers.

In the course of this violence, some kin groups did better than others. Those that prevailed formed ruling lineages and provided kings. Central to the emergence of these monarchies—and central, therefore, to the emergence of the state—was the alliance between militarized lineages and the new economic order. Driven by necessity, fighting lineages allied with the cities, using them as a source of finance with which to suppress and seduce elites in the countryside, and so transforming the political structure of Europe.

PREDATION

To pay for their wars, the heads of ruling lineages broke into the strongholds of subjects to seize gold and jewels placed there for safekeeping. They confiscated the wealth of their bankers, the estates of the church, and possessions of their aristocrats. And they attempted to live off the bounty that they could seize through fighting. "The great series of campaigns launched in Aquitaine, Brittany, and Normandy after 1341," it is said, became a "'joint-stock' enterprise" in which resources were ventured in expectation of subsequent shares (Ormrod 1990, 103).

In search of revenues with which to finance their military ventures, monarchs also tapped the income generated on their own lands. They sold timber from their forests; grazed livestock and grew grain; and excavated minerals from beneath their farms. They recruited and settled tenants on their domains, hired estate managers and supervisors; and, by collecting dues and fees, extracted income from the royal demesne.

Seeking to pay for their wars, the heads of ruling families also manipulated the rules of kinship. In pursuit of economic resources, monarchs charged fees for permission to marry. They sought to impose self-serving definitions of the rules of descent, demanding payment by sons to keep the lands of their fathers. And when those too young or too weak to meet their political obligations inherited estates, they became wards of the king; his bureaucrats then managed their lands, collecting incomes from them, or placed them under the control of those who allied with the king. By manipulating the rules of kinship, those with power thus acquired wealth and property in Europe's agrarian economy, and the resources by which to finance their battles.

SEDUCTION

In search of finances, monarchs also turned to the wealth of the towns. But in their efforts to prey upon the wealth of the urban centers, they found seduction preferable to bullying as a means of securing revenues.

Urban centers could better defend themselves than could rural centers of power. Both a walled town and a castle could neutralize armed horsemen. But, in the face of the use of cannon, cities possessed an advantage. Endowed with greater wealth and numbers, they could construct protective embankments to absorb a projectile's shock. The rural warlord lacked comparable resources and a comparable level of defense.

Not only was it therefore difficult to seize a town; but the benefits were few. Because of the mobility of urban assets, the physical seizure of the towns yielded few rewards. In England, for example, Edward II broke into the vaults of the Knights Templars to seize gold and plate, and thus finance his wars; centuries later, Charles I seized gold that had been deposited for safekeeping in the Tower. But Londoners then simply moved their wealth, transferring it from central points of storage to the vaults of private goldsmiths scattered about town. And in the mid-sixteenth century, the Spanish army benefited little from seizing Antwerp, as the merchants and those that financed them simply decamped to Amsterdam. The short-term benefits of preying upon cities therefore came at high cost; and because urbanites could reallocate their wealth so as to elude predation by monarchs, the benefits proved few.

In the face of the urban economy, specialists in violence therefore had to alter their strategies for securing revenues. In the words of Montesquieu, the monarchs had "to govern with greater wisdom than they themselves had intended" (quoted in Hirschman 1977, 72). Rather than plundering wealth, they had instead to elicit its creation. They had to nurture, rather than to despoil, the new economy. They had to adopt policies that facilitated the growth of towns.

Protection   Under what is called "mercantilism," ruling lineages actively promoted the growth of manufacturing in towns.

They limited the importation of finished goods, thus protecting local manufacturers from competition from abroad. By imposing tariffs and quotas on the import of textiles, cloth, fabrics, and other items, they allowed the prices of these goods to rise. Governments also limited the exportation of raw materials; by placing barriers on the export of wood, iron, copper, fibers, and other items used in manufacturing, they reduced the domestic price of the raw materials used by urban industry. These mercantilist policies—raising prices for finished products and reducing the costs of production—increased the profits that could be earned by manufacturers in town.

Not only did ruling lineages protect manufacturers from competition from abroad; they also protected them from competition in the domestic market. Particularly in France, the government licensed the production of key consumer goods, restricting the privilege of their manufacture to master craftsmen and their guilds. By regulating apprenticeships and training, and by imposing restrictions on the materials used and the processes employed by manufacturers, they restricted entry, limited output, and thereby created the power to raise prices above the level that would have prevailed in competitive markets.

Procurement   Governments also promoted the fortunes of urban manufacturers by lowering the costs of food and raw materials. Whereas the producers of textiles and other manufactured goods received protection from imports, the producers of grain, fibers, timber, and other products received none. Urban dwellers, who consumed the food, and manufacturers, who used the raw materials, could thus purchase the products of agriculture at the lowest prices available, be it at home or abroad.

Policies of "provisioning" illustrate the favor shown urban industry. Governments built and maintained warehouses; superintended marketing of grain and the baking of bread; and oversaw the purchase, storage, and distribution of food. While allowing the restriction of supplies by urban manufacturers, they branded similar efforts by merchants and farmers as "forestalling," declaring it a violation of law. Governments thus intervened in agricultural markets in ways that lowered prices to urban consumers and enhanced the fortunes of those employed in urban industry.

Government policies thus enhanced the profits of urban industry. Promoting on the one hand "high price" policies for manufactured goods, governments took measures on the other that lowered the prices paid by urban dwellers for goods purchased from agriculture. The resultant increase in revenues and decrease in costs enhanced the profits of those in town.

Empowerment   A third measure that characterized the mercantilist policies of government was the exchange of the right to govern for the payment of taxes. Monarchs permitted urban centers to purchase their "liberties"; by making payments to the treasury, merchants and burghers could purchase charters from the king that granted them the authority to make and enforce laws, construct public works, set and collect local taxes, and allocate public revenues.

In most instances, to be a "citizen" of a town, a person had to be a member of a guild; he had to be a member of an association of merchants or artisans who specialized in a particular trade. The delegation of power to the citizens of the towns thus constituted a conferral of power upon the members of industries.

Viewed one way, the charters provide confirmation of the favorable bargaining position of the towns; the liberty of the towns provides visible evidence of the political limits that they could impose upon resource-starved kings. Viewed another way, the charters do not signal a negative check upon monarchical power; rather, they suggest a positive political investment. The investment was not of wealth; instead, it was of power. By delegating to the citizens of the towns the power to govern their affairs, the monarchs empowered them to form economic organizations capable of promoting the growth of the urban economy—and thus the government's revenue base.

The managers of the affairs of the industries used these powers to promote the formation of capital. Through the apprenticeship system, they restricted competition in the labor market; they also shaped the time profile of wages, so that the master craftsmen paid low wages to those in training and higher wages to workers when fully skilled. By thus organizing the market for labor, the guilds rendered credible the employees' pledges that, were their employers to invest in their training, they would not then defect to the workshop of a competitor. The regulations on apprenticeship therefore strengthened the capacity of industry to upgrade the skills of its workers.

The industrialists also used their power to build reputations for their products, thus promoting their sale at home and their export abroad. Under the powers conferred by the municipal charters, they prescribed the use of particular inputs and the use of particular production methods. They thereby sought to prevent "chiselers" from profiting from the use of lower-cost methods to produce goods of lower quality, which they could then market under the "brand name" built by others. By securing the power to threaten sanctions, urban manufacturers secured the capacity to create a reputation for quality.

The industrial organizations took further steps to shape the conduct of their members. They created offices and ceremonial positions that were deeply desired. By creating such posts, they rendered prominence and standing conditional on not only private wealth but also the provision of public service. The guilds maintained lodges and common eating-places for their members and organized collective activities, such as celebrations of saints' days, pageants, festivals, and feasts. Their officeholders regulated life in the halls and commons of the guild. And they acted as policemen and regulators, prosecuting malefactors in industrial courts. Among the greatest of the penalties they imposed was expulsion from the fellowship of the community—and from the trade it organized.

The liberties conferred on towns thus put the power of the state in the service of nascent industries, and of the communities built up around them. By investing their power in the hands of urban "citizens," the monarchs enhanced their capacity to organize productive activity. And by exchanging money for liberty, the towns helped to increase the revenues of the monarch.

ON THE ONE HAND, mercantilism constituted a cluster of policies aimed at the promotion of urban manufacturing; on the other, it constituted a means for paying for the king's wars. Powerful ties of self-interest ran from the making of wars to the search for revenues and thence to the promotion of urban-based economic activity. The desire to prevail—and the necessity of prevailing—in combat shaped the economic role of government in the development of Europe.

PEACEKEEPING

The rise of manufacturing promoted the growth not only of towns, but also of rural economies. The increase in rural wealth produced in its train an increase in private violence, and the formation of private armies, led by rural elites, that sought to encroach upon the wealth of others. The demilitarization of these kinship groups took place when, on the one hand, rural dwellers came to demand it and, on the other, monarchs could afford to impose order.

THE DEMAND

With the commercialization of agriculture, land became valuable and fighting therefore increased; such conflicts, once launched, were difficult to terminate. Fighting interrupted farming and destroyed crops, livestock, property, and human life. With the rise in demand for rural products, peace became increasingly valuable. Evidence is provided by the behavior of rural magnates in the Parliament of England, who repeatedly put forward proposals for rural disarmament: they approved bills calling for the disbanding of liveried companies—groups of warriors, wearing their colors, that they themselves had originally assembled (Hicks 1995, 128). On the Continent, local notables and clergy organized peace movements, calling on monarchs to enter their troubled districts and to put an end to the fighting (Duby 1991, 187ff).

In England, where the process has perhaps best been studied, monarchs responded by mobilizing the local system of justice. Under the system of the feud, kin possessed a collective obligation to revenge wrongs inflicted upon one of their members; under the system advanced by the monarchs, they again bore collective responsibility, but now to surrender one of their members had he inflicted a wrong upon others. Failing the surrender of the offender, the kin group itself then became subject to the mercy of the king. The new system thus tapped into the social structures that had animated the old; however, it altered the incentives that governed these structures, resulting not in reprisals and further fighting but in the apprehension of felons and their delivery to the courts of the king.

The system of private justice had inflicted losses, not only in terms of physical damage but also in terms of uncertainty and delay, as disputes reverberated through time. The new system too posed dangers, most notably that of generating decisions and rulings of low quality. While those who imposed law and order made efforts to inform themselves, as by empaneling juries, they were nonetheless outsiders and therefore less likely to possess the detailed information than would neighbors and kin. Given the possibility for costly mistakes, the preference for the new system derived not from the accuracy of the outcomes it rendered, then, but rather from their speed. Particularly in disputes over land, the system was designed to deliver quick rulings.[1]

Providing grain, meat, timber, and above all wool to the towns, England's farmlands generated such a high rate of growth of income that rural dwellers desired rapid adjudication, even if it might yield unfavorable settlements. This growth in the earnings to be gained from farming, then, appears to have led to a preference for a system that generated rapid outcomes, freighted with possible losses, over one that may have been better able to generate correct outcomes, but ones long delayed. It led to increased demands for an official system of justice and a willingness to pay for it. The court fees collected by the king more than covered the costs of the legal system, and fees from the provision of justice soon grew into a major source of government revenues.

It is notable that during the creation of the new political order, criminal law became separate from civil. Rather than

---

[1] And where the parties sought such accelerated rulings, they had first to agree not to appeal the resulting decisions. Note the discussion of "novel desseisin" in Hudson (1996).

being subject to civil proceedings, with possibilities for compensation and the reconciliation of the contending parties, murder, assault, and grievous attacks were now defined as crimes. They were treated as offenses against the state. The threat of revenge and physical reprisal had lain at the heart of the private provision of security. The redefinition of such acts as felonies thus signaled a fundamental recasting of the political systems and a step in the demilitarization of kin groups in rural communities.

THE SUPPLY

Upon assuming the throne, Henry I proclaimed: "I place strong peace on all my kingdom and order it to be held henceforth" (quoted in Hudson 1996, 82). As he, like other monarchs, learned, however, peace cannot be simply proclaimed. Rather, it has to be organized. On the "supply side," the monarch had to deploy coercion and inducements—things he was now better positioned to provide, given his access to new sources of income.

Repression   The demobilization of kin groups and communities required careful coordination. No party dared unilaterally disarm. And once a party did disarm, it could no longer threaten lethal reprisals. Just at the point where arms were to be surrendered, then, each was most reluctant and most vulnerable.

In situations so laden with distrust, it was therefore crucial that each party to a dispute be able to depend upon the power of the king. In particular, it was crucial that each believe that the king could, and would, hunt and harry those who might violate the peace. It was crucial that each party believe that the king was so powerful that no one would emerge unscathed should he renege upon an agreement forged in the process of pacification.

With their growing access to the wealth of the new economy, monarchs were able to assemble armies of sufficient size and power to provide the assurances necessary to demilitarize kin groups and communities. While rural warlords may have been able to mobilize retainers, the monarch could pay for armies, train them, and keep them in the field. Private armies could feud; those of the monarch could campaign. As a result, the monarch possessed the power to impose "the institution of the peace," as it was known: "Everyone living [under the institution] was strictly bound to keep the peace. . . . Agreements of this kind were gradually established, point by point, across the country by the king" (Duby 1991, 141).

Seduction   As previously noted, elites had already expressed weariness with fighting, passing legislation that imposed limits on private armies. The interests of the rural elite often failed to coincide with those of their retainers. Obligated to punish for harms inflicted upon members of their households, local warlords found themselves, in the words of Hicks, "drawn into conflicts on issues of little concern to themselves" (1995, 151). From the monarch's point of view, the elites were therefore ripe for co-optation. Once again, the wealth of the monarchs came to play an important role in the reorganization of violence.

Replete with revenues, the court had become a fountain of privilege (see Peck 1990; Root 1994). By judiciously targeting her favors, the monarch could make, or break, the fortunes of a clan head, and so render it in the interests of agrarian elites to withdraw from their rural redoubts and to attach themselves to the center. In this manner, too, kings secured the demobilization of the countryside.

An example is provided by the taming of the Percys, who had long intrigued with rivals to the English throne, helping to split the royal lineage and threaten the reigns of the Plantagenets and Lancasters alike. Throughout much of England's history, the cry "A Percy, a Percy," arising in the north, spread fear throughout the south, even in the court of the king. As the revenues of the monarch swelled, however, so too did the king's capacity to tame the Percy clan. The monarch showered favors upon its members, leasing them crown property on favorable terms, bequeathing to them the estates of traitors or estates in conquered lands, and conferring upon them annuities, fee farms, and trading privileges. As with other local clans, the Percys found their fortunes increasingly dependent upon their ties to the throne (Stone 1965, 250ff).

Those that the monarch thus favored, the monarch could also destroy. When Elizabeth I turned against Robert Devereux, Earl of Essex, for example, she first canceled his monopoly on imports of sweet wine. Without this monopoly, Essex could no longer secure credit from banks or acquaintances; he therefore had to dismiss his retainers, reduce his household, and retire from the court (Stone 1965, 481ff).[2]

In sixteenth-century England, when the monarch surveyed the political landscape, she saw Bedford in the southwest, Pembroke in Wales, Arundel in Sussex, Norfolk in East Anglia, Derby in the northwest, and Northumberland in the northeast. By the seventeenth century, each magnate and his family had been defeated or seduced by the center. Possessing greater revenues, the monarchy mobilized greater force. And by channeling wealth through politics, the monarch was able to transform the behavior of rural kin groups; when their standing came to depend less upon "territorial power than upon influence in

---

[2] It is important to note that not only did the Tudors use the conferral and withdrawal of privileges to domesticate the Percys and Essex, they also used their power to coerce. Elizabeth savagely crushed the last of the Percy rebellions, and had Essex executed for treason.

London" (Stone 1965, 257), the heads of such groups invested less in rural domination and more in playing the game of court politics.

The economic transformation of the countryside thus inspired a quest for new ways of structuring political life. In response to the demands for peace, monarchs transformed the local order, demilitarizing kinship, co-opting elites, and incorporating local communities into a system that terminated, rather than exacerbated, conflict. Creating the rudiments of what we now call a state, those that headed the dominant lineages restructured the use of violence.

THE LEGENDS, BALLADS, AND POETRY that depict the process of state making emphasize several major themes. One is that of betrayal, as elites callously abandon rural retainers while turning their energies to the more profitable prospects offered by kings and courts. In Japan, we encounter tales of wandering samurai, whose services were no longer needed or honored by their clans; in Great Britain, we encounter the lamentations of the Scots, whose chiefs abandoned warfare for farming, cleared their lands of retainers, and forced kin and dependents to quit their homelands for settlement abroad. Henry V, once he became king, let Falstaff hang. Memories of abandonment darken the glow that infuses romantic images of a life before the great transformation.

As illustrated by *The Song of Roland*, which celebrates the royal lineage of medieval France, the literature of state building advances a second theme. The ballad recalls how, in the midst of battle, Ganelon, like Roland in service to Charlemagne, seized an opportunity for private vengeance and, in so doing, placed the army of the king in mortal peril. Put on trial for his actions, Ganelon appeals to the code of family honor. While initially appearing to be swayed by his appeals, his jurors end by rejecting his defense and convict him of treason.[3]

The change in the position of Ganelon's peers marks a shift from the ethic of vengeance. It proclaims the arrival of a new political order—one based not upon the private provision of violence, but rather upon the public provision of force. Reading the ballad, one notes that violence has not been ended; Ganelon dies a horrible death. But with the rise of the state, coercion is now deployed for new purposes.

In historical Europe, then, states emerged from war. Governments pursued policies that promoted the development of the economy not because they wanted to but because they had to, the better to secure the resources with which to fight. As states developed, coercion did not disappear. Rather, when those who specialized in its use altered the purposes to which they employed it, coercion provided the political foundations for the great transformation.

[3] See Anonymous (1990). *The Forty-seven Ronins* explores a similar conflict of loyalties in early modern Japan (Mitford 1966).

4

STATE FORMATION
IN THE MODERN ERA

There mark what ills . . . life assail,
Toil, envy, want, the patron, and the jail
—SAMUEL JOHNSON, *THE VANITY*
OF HUMAN WISHES, LINES 159–60

IN THE PREVIOUS CHAPTERS, we have learned that the development of the European nations was animated by warfare abroad and the search at home for revenues with which to pay for fighting. In this we shall see that the midcentury emergence of the developing nations took place in a global system in which great powers, out of a regard for their own interests, policed conflicts in the periphery and consolidated their influence by transferring resources to the developing nations. These differences in the interstate system, I argue, have imparted a distinctive character to development in the modern era.

Although divided among themselves, the vast majority of those who have studied developing societies concur that the experiences of the states born after World War II differ from those of states that developed before them, if only because the "early developers" dominate their international environments. I heartily agree with this position. I decidedly dissent, however, from the oft-stated corollary that the relative poverty and weakness of the developing nations accounts for, and indeed underpins, their choice of economic policies. The differences run deeper than that, I argue, and affect the very institutions and structures within which these policies are devised and chosen.

ECONOMIC POLICY

Ironically, given the argument of most development specialists, the economic policies of the developing nations bear a striking resemblance to the mercantilist policies of their predecessors.

Following the attainment of independence, the governments of most developing countries adopted policies of import-substituting industrialization. By banning imports of manufactured goods, they strengthened the incentives for investors to create enterprises that would manufacture goods locally. Encouraged by such policies, owners of capital invested in the local production of shoes, clothing, processed foods, blankets, vegetable oils, building materials, bicycles, and other goods that hitherto had been imported from abroad.

FAVORING INDUSTRY

Governments protected domestic industries by restricting foreign competition and sheltered them from local competition as well. To strengthen incentives for investment, they restricted entry into markets, conferring monopoly rights upon favored local firms, or upon firms owned by the government itself.

To promote domestic industry, governments also adopted policies that lowered the prices of raw materials. Grains, fibers, food, and timber could be imported freely, should their prices abroad lie below those in the domestic market. Should their prices abroad lie above those in the domestic market, however, then their export was banned. Producers of palm oil were thus compelled to sell their products to local manufacturers, even if the latter offered prices lower than those being offered abroad. The growers of sisal and jute found their options limited, out of a regard for the promotion of local producers of twine and rope. As a result of possessing a captive market, local manufacturers could pay lower prices for their raw materials, and thereby secure higher profits.

Just as governments in Europe had keyed their domestic bureaucracies to the delivery of low-cost grain to their growing industrial centers, so too did modern developing nations create bureaucracies to accumulate, warehouse, and distribute food at prices favorable to urban consumers. City dwellers; civil servants, particularly in the capital; and the armed forces—all became the clients of these bureaucracies. Those whose job it was to insure domestic security often superintended the distribution of food: for example, in Zambia, the Office of the President or, in Kenya, the Provincial Administration.

FOUNTAIN OF PRIVILEGE

To promote development, then, governments sought to promote the formation of urban-based industry. By actively intervening in the economy, they, like their mercantilist predecessors, also rendered the government a "fountain of privilege." In Indonesia, for example, the government enabled President Suharto's family to accumulate extraordinary fortunes from their part ownership of a "skein of companies" (over five hundred in all) whose fortunes were favored by state policy. Suharto's government allocated to his children, his military allies, and their political favorites the right to control exports of oil, timber, and minerals, and the right to control the import of plastics, arms, and spare parts. His government pressured banks to offer low-rate loans to political favorites, and made it unwise for them to call in such loans, even when repayment was not forthcoming. The family and its friends reportedly "own[ed] or through corporate entities control[ed] some 3.6 million hectares of real estate in Indonesia, an area larger than Belgium."[1]

The activist policies of Kenya's post-independence government provide another illustration. Sons, daughters, and wives of President Jomo Kenyatta acquired loans, concessions, and properties, including ranches in the highlands, estates in the coffee zones, houses in Nairobi, and hotels on the beaches of the Indian Ocean. Kenyatta's government exempted presidential favorites from the Land Control Act, thus allowing them to develop commercial property on public lands, including Kenya's famous game reserves. With subsidized loans from the state agricultural bank, some purchased estates from white settlers and formed a landowning class in the highlands. With subsidized loans from the state commercial bank, others acquired franchises from multinational corporations and the sole right to import and to distribute their products. With subsidized loans from the state industrial bank, still others launched firms to produce clothing, shoes, and bottled drinks—products sheltered from foreign competition by tariffs and from domestic competition by licensing agreements.

Just as had monarchs in European states, so too do presi-

[1] *Time* (Asia), May 24, 1999, p. 12.

dents in newly independent states use the economic power of the state not only to reward but also to punish. I recall working in western Kenya shortly after Daniel arap Moi succeeded Jomo Kenyatta as president of Kenya. With the shift in power, the political fortunes of elite politicians had changed. As I drove through the highlands, I encountered boldly lettered signs posted on the gateways of farms announcing the auction of cattle, farm machinery, and buildings and lands. Once they were no longer in favor, politicians found their loans canceled or called in, their subsidies withdrawn, or their lines of business, which had once been sheltered by the state, exposed to competition. Some whom I had once seen in the hotels of Nairobi, looking sleek and satisfied, I now encountered in rural bars, looking lean and apprehensive, as they contemplated the magnitude of their reversal.

To promote development, modern governments have sought to industrialize. Their policies of import-substituting industrialization created firms, companies, projects, and ventures, as well as an economically privileged class whose fortunes depended upon political favor. Critics of Jean-Baptiste Colbert, the leading proponent of mercantilism, once stated of the guilds that these "corporations are like links in a great chain whose beginning lies in [your] hands" (Heckscher 1955, 217). So too did the policies of modern governments enable them to place supporters in profitable niches in the new economy, and thus to tie local elites to the political center.

In the modern literature on development, scholars emphasize the impact upon the developing economy of those economies that are already developed. The economic power of the one distorts the economic policies of the other, it is claimed. But this review of the policies of the modern-day developing societies finds them to have resembled, to a striking degree, the policies of the advanced developing states when they themselves were developing.

DIFFERENCES

If not decisively impacting upon the economic policies of the developing nations, the postwar global structure of power did impact upon their political structures, and in ways that profoundly affected their development. The international system limited the use of force abroad and provided international sources of state revenues. It thereby shaped the manner in which ruling elites in the developing world governed in the postwar period and the nature of the institutions that they forged in so doing.

THE INTERNATIONAL SYSTEM

The nations of Europe emerged from the Second World War crippled by years of fighting. So desperate had the conflict been that they had pledged political independence to their colonies in exchange for assistance in the fighting; and so financially exhausted were they that after the war they were unable to renege on those promises. The Soviet Union and the United States emerged from the conflict as the sole remaining global powers. Both could mobilize heavy industry for war; both possessed nuclear weapons. Given the resources that each could marshal, their rivalry engulfed the globe.

There is no government at the international level, and the conflicts between the Soviet Union and the United States resembled those that characterize societies without states. Each political champion led a "family," i.e., a network of dependents and allies; each possessed a "neighborhood," Eastern Europe in the one instance, Latin and Central America in the other. The security system put in place after World War II took as its premise the territorial integrity of states. Just as the infringement upon a family's property might trigger reprisal in kinship systems, so the infringement of territorial sovereignty might now trigger responses in the international system. The pattern of political order thus resembled that of a feud.

Given the absence of an international government, security in the global system, as in a kinship system, flowed from the capacity to utter threats that were credible and so able to deter aggression. The dangers posed by this system therefore also resembled those that mark kinship systems: small transgressions could trigger costly conflicts, as agents sought to preserve the credibility of their reputations. Both the Soviet Union and the United States prized their holdings in the advanced industrial world. Neither placed comparable value on their stakes in the less developed periphery. While willing to risk incinerating the world in a fight over Berlin, neither wished to do so in a dispute over Bamako. It was therefore in the interests of the global powers to invest in means of peacekeeping, and, indeed, they joined in creating institutions that would reduce the likelihood of their coming to blows in what they regarded as the more remote regions of the globe.

The great powers created the United Nations as a means of reducing that danger. Through the Security Council, they could brand a conflict as a possible threat to international peace and security; the United Nations could then provide peacekeeping facilities, be it envoys, mediators, or armed forces. By enabling the great powers to dampen the possible escalation of small disputes, the United Nations thereby defended their interests; it limited their involvement in disputes of marginal interest to them.

The newly independent nations that emerged after World War II might not have possessed military bureaucracies capable of fighting wars, financial bureaucracies capable of securing stable economies or growth, or internal governments capable of demilitarizing kinship systems and local communities. They might, then, not in fact have been states. But in order to lower political tensions and to promote global peace, they were proclaimed sovereign nations, within the structure of political institutions created after the war.

THE REVENUE IMPERATIVE

Many of the states that took part in World War II had been created in the early modern period and had been born of fighting. By contrast, the postwar system checked the military impulse of the newly independent nations. The developing nations faced a global environment that differed from that of their predecessors in another critical respect: foreign sources of state finance were abundant, by comparison with those available to their predecessors. The states lay imbedded in international lines of patronage that ramified from Washington and Moscow. Some were paid *not* to fight. These differences in the nature of the interstate system shaped the nature of these states and the properties of their institutions.

Early Modern States   In an effort to finance their wars, European monarchs had sought to extract higher levels of resources from their domestic economies. Both to tax and to borrow, they found it necessary to restructure their relationships with those whom they asked to bear the costs of government. The economic imperative—the need for resources and the necessity of raising them domestically—became a political imperative, shaping their institutions of government.

In search of funds with which to finance their armies, monarchs extended the tax base from "real property" to "movables": articles that could be traded, transported, or hidden (Prestwich 1972; Mitchell 1951). Taxes on movables could readily be evaded; to secure payment, the monarch therefore needed the cooperation of those who owned such property. As the costs of war grew, wise monarchs therefore chose their military ventures with an eye to the opinions of the taxpayers, the better to elicit support for their policies and to strengthen their willingness to pay for them (Rosenthal 1998).

When military intervention needed to be ratified in order to be financed, then, too, it was necessary that those who approved such ventures enter the bargaining *plena potesta*—i.e., fully empowered to bind their communities. Such institutions as civilian oversight, commoner councils, and parliamentary forms of government provided means for contracting between the owners of private assets, who supplied revenues, and the specialists in violence, who demanded them to finance their wars. These forms of representation were thus an institutional by-product of the effort to transform private wealth into public revenues.

Wars imparted sharp shocks to the economy, the magnitudes of which increased with the sophistication of the instruments of combat. Monarchs could not hope to wring from their economies the resources necessary to cover the full costs of a war. What monarchs could not raise through taxation, they therefore sought to borrow.

When governments needed loans, the loans were of much greater magnitude than those required by private borrowers. The debts incurred in private commerce were short-term, often merely serving to cover a distinct transaction. By contrast, the debts of government were of long duration: at least that of a military campaign, and sometimes that of a protracted conflict. In addition, loans to commerce could be made at low risk: lenders could seize the goods of a debtor. But loans to government were made at greater risk: monarchs, being sovereign, could renege on their obligations to repay.

To increase the willingness of those with capital to lend it, governments therefore sought ways to offer security to their creditors. They allowed bankers to become "tax farmers," collectors of customs or the managers of conquered territories; title to the taxes and incomes provided security for their loans to the treasury. Alternatively, monarchs granted monopolies to their creditors; assured of high profits from monopolies created by the government, chartered companies and licensed purveyors were willing to run the risks of lending. Such measures went only partway in addressing the concerns of investors, however, for just as monarchs could renege on their debts, so too might they abrogate such agreements. The costs of borrowing therefore remained high, because creditors demanded compensation for lending large amounts for long duration to governments that could renege with impunity.

Insofar as European governments "solved" the problem of financing public debt, they did so by building upon the same institutions that they had forged to levy taxes, i.e., upon their assemblies. Seventeenth-century England offers the most compelling example. As had the Habsburgs before them, the French coveted the wealth of the lowlands; the Dutch therefore feared the renewal of war. Surveying the polity that lay across the Channel, the Dutch spied both opportunity and danger. They noted the wealth of the English economy. But they were disturbed by the danger posed by the polity, and in particular, by the Stuarts, the ruling lineage, who possessed religious preferences and financial needs that rendered them susceptible to pressures from France. Building a fleet that rivaled in size the Spanish Armada, Dutch invaders joined English opponents to Stuart rule, drove the Stuarts from the throne, and replaced them with their own ruling family, the House of Orange. The House of Orange had long since learned how to finance, to raise, and to equip a disciplined army. The Dutch polity consisted of a federation of urban-based assemblies. The most efficient way to mobilize revenues, its ruling family had learned, was through parliaments.

To address the concerns of creditors, William of Orange therefore agreed to the sovereignty of England's Parliament, which meant, in this context, two specific things. The first was parliamentary control over policy: he, the specialist in violence, would fight only those wars that Parliament would consent to fund. The second was parliamentary control over public finances, which implied control over both taxation and the financing of the public debt. In effect, those who controlled the wealth of the nation now would have to finance only those ventures for which they were willing to pay. Having surrendered sovereignty to those who controlled the private economy, the monarch could no longer capriciously make, and break, promises. By limiting his power, the monarch enhanced his credit and so lowered the costs of borrowing. As canny in devising political solutions to financial problems as they were in fighting wars, the Dutch transformed English political institutions in ways that gave political assurances to investors and augmented the flow of capital to the state and revenues to its army.

The need to secure finances from citizens—through taxation and public debt—in order to pay for wars therefore produced a characteristic structure of political institutions in the early modern state.

The Developing Nations   The blunting of the military imperative in the developing world led to a relationship between political elites and the citizenry that differ from what had evolved in Europe. The governments of the developing nations were less likely to view their economies as a strategic resource, to be nurtured and burnished as if a ship or gun. There were, of course, exceptions: both the Japanese, who overthrew the Tokugawa empire, and the Turks, who overthrew the empire of the Ottomans, sought to forge states capable of repelling foreign military threats. To secure military security, they sought to build a strong economy, capable of financing armed forces of sufficient strength to give pause to those with greater power. But few other governments felt similarly driven to fortify their political economies or to make economic policy out of a regard for international security.

An additional reason for refraining from the generation of resources at home was that, by exploiting Cold War rivalries, the governments of developing nations could secure revenue from abroad. When Cuba allied with the Soviet Union, for example, then the United States massively increased its development assistance to the nations of Latin America. Originally a security alliance, the Organization of American States (OAS) became a forum for the propounding and financing of development programs. Within the OAS, the United States forged the Alliance for Progress with Latin America, designed both to assist in the development of the region and to secure the political backing of its governments.

Similar patterns prevailed in other portions of the globe. To counter the threat of Soviet influence in Africa, for example, the United States backed the rise to power of Joseph Désiré Mobutu, who overthrew an incumbent regime that was unwilling or unable to counter radical forces in the Congo. Provoked by the rising opposition to South Africa's white minority regime, politicians in neighboring states increasingly sought support from China, Russia, and Cuba. By contrast, Mobutu (who later changed his name to Mobutu Sese Seko) increasingly benefited from his steadfast willingness to oppose their initiatives. He received increased amounts of aid in return for offering a safe haven for the opponents of Angola's socialist regime and for allowing the use of his territory to arm those who fought Cuba's forces in southern Africa.

Under Mobutu's rule, the road system of Zaire disintegrated; its teachers and civil servants remained, for months, unpaid; its hospitals, clinics, and schools decayed; its agricultural exports collapsed; its rich mines barely functioned. Nevertheless, the United States continued to finance Mobutu and his government, enabling them to survive, even while destroying the economy of their nation.

During the Cold War, the United States was often criticized for supporting regimes in power that violated its democratic principles. As illustrated by the case of Mobutu, the government did indeed often ally itself with dictators and authoritarians. While hypocrisy certainly played its part, this analysis points to deeper forces. Propped up by the forces unleashed by the Cold War, local elites in the developing world did not fear falling, should they become unpopular; nor, supported by transfers of aid from abroad, did they need to bargain with their citizens to secure public revenues. They therefore did not need to be responsive to their people or democratic in their politics, for want of the kinds of pressures that in the past had compelled governments to become democracies. The United States may not have been attracted to dictators, then; rather, it may have created them, or at least arrested the forces of accountability that in an earlier era might have made them democratic.

THE OLDER STATES WERE BORN of war. In search of funds, monarchs devised ways to persuade those who earned private incomes to pay the costs of government and, by rendering credible their promises to repay, to assume the government's debts. To enhance their security abroad, kings forged political arrangements at home that enhanced the willingness of those with capital to finance the costs of government. The creation of liberal political institutions was thus a by-product of the impact of military insecurity upon the need for government revenues.

The international environment faced by the developing world in the postwar period generated few incentives to behave in such ways. The high politics of the developing areas did not take the form of heads of state confronting their people, seeking ways to get them to pay for the costs of government. The military threat was less and foreign sources of capital more abundant. The governments of developing nations therefore faced fewer incentives to forge liberal political institutions. The international system may not have led to a choice of policies that differed from those of early modern states in Europe, but it did yield a different structure of politics.

5

LATE-CENTURY
SHOCKS TO THE
GLOBAL SYSTEM

. . . where peace
And rest can never dwell, hope never comes
—JOHN MILTON, *PARADISE LOST*,
BOOK I, LINES 65–66

ACHIEVING INDEPENDENCE in the midst of the twentieth
century, the developing nations entered into an economic and
political system shaped by the conflict between the two great
powers. However, in the last two decades of the twentieth century, the global environment profoundly altered. In the early
1980s, shocks to the international economy precipitated a crisis
of debt; less than a decade later, the collapse of the Soviet Union
put an end to the Cold War. These changes in the international
system impacted deeply upon the economic policies of developing nations, the nature of their politics, and the structure of
their institutions.

In the face of the debt crisis, the options open to the developing nations changed. Governments were compelled more tightly to limit their spending and to adopt more liberal economic policies. In the face of the end of the Cold War, the advanced industrial nations placed a lower priority on checking the spread of violence in the developing world. The result of the debt crisis and the end of the Cold War was to produce a change in economic policies and to alter domestic patterns of politics.

Three literatures address the political changes in the last decades of the twentieth century. One focuses on policy reform; the other two on democratization and violence. This chapter posits the existence of strong linkages among the three phenomena and argues that they can be beneficially explored together. They find common ground, I argue, in the late-century shocks to the global system.

THE CHANGING ECONOMIC CONTEXT

In the early 1980s, the global economy fell into recession and the developing world into a crisis of debt. One source of the debt crisis lay within the developing world itself and stemmed from the content of their development policies; others lay outside the control of the developing nations. I turn first to their development policies.

The governments of the newly independent nations had sought to secure foreign investments by placing barriers on imports, seeking thereby to induce foreign corporations to import manufacturing plants and equipment that would enable them to make goods locally. The protection thus afforded led, of course, to higher prices in domestic markets. Exporters found that, given the higher prices, they could purchase less with their foreign earnings and the incentive to export therefore declined. The very policies that encouraged the increased importation of plant and equipment, then, rendered the developing nations short of foreign exchange and dependent upon credit from abroad.

The economic policies of the developing nations thus rendered them structurally dependent upon foreign capital. The actions of other nations—in particular, the oil-exporting nations—further weakened their standing in global markets. In the 1970s, the oil-producing nations twice increased the price of their exports. Their targets had been the developed economies of the West, whose industries consumed massive amounts of energy and whose wealthy inhabitants had, they felt, for too long paid too little for oil. While the Western nations may have been the intended victims of these price rises, many developing countries, themselves importers of petroleum, also stood in harm's way. Indeed, they suffered doubly: once from the higher costs of petroleum imports and once again from a reduction in their exports, as the advanced industrial economies, staggered by the higher costs of energy, reduced their consumption of other goods, including those exported by the developing nations.

Policies of import substitution had already placed at risk the trade balances of the developing nations. The massive increases in petroleum prices heightened the peril. Ironically, however, the very crisis that had placed the developing nations in danger also temporarily alleviated their problem. The solution proved short-term, however, and indeed increased the severity of the subsequent economic collapse.

Rather than having their newfound riches sit idle, the oil-exporting states placed them in banks, which then on-lent them in international credit markets. Among the customers of these banks were governments of developing nations, who sought loans that would enable them to continue their development programs, even in the face of higher oil prices. Initially, the costs of such borrowing remained low. Capital was abundant and therefore cheap. And rampant inflation in the United States meant that debts contracted at one point in time could later be repaid in dollars of lesser value. In the face of their need for foreign capital—generated both by the nature of their development programs and by the higher costs of oil— the developing countries therefore faced an international banking system awash with dollars that could be borrowed on favorable terms. And borrow many did, further increasing their levels of debt.

What caused the developing nations to default, foreign creditors to retreat, and thus the actual debt crisis was an abrupt increase in the costs of borrowing, sparked by a sharp rise in interest rates. Determined to put an end to inflation in the United States, Paul Volcker, chairman of the Federal Reserve System, radically raised the rate of interest in United States markets. His actions provoked a sharp recession in the U.S. economy. With recession in the United States, exports to the world's biggest market declined, resulting in a shortage of dollars with which to repay foreign loans. And with the end of inflation and a rise in the real rate of interest, the costs of debt repayment rose.

In August 1982 Mexico announced its inability to meet its obligations to its creditors; consulting their books, bankers realized that the problems faced by Mexico confronted many other nations as well. Fearing further defaults, private sources therefore ceased lending to developing countries. Much of the developing world could no longer borrow, even to repay past loans. Taken together, the structural stresses arising from the policies of import substitution, increased prices for oil and capital, and then the Mexican default, which caused panic among foreign lenders, radically altered the economic environment faced by the developing nations.

CHANGES IN THE POLITICAL CONTEXT

As Soviet troops moved toward Berlin at the end of World War II, they occupied the nations of Eastern Europe and stood guard while Communist parties seized control of their governments. Even in nations that escaped Soviet occupation, Communist parties remained a formidable presence, nearly seizing power in Greece and commanding large blocs of supporters in Italy and France. The political influence of the Soviet Union thus extended beyond the reach of its armed forces. To combat Soviet influence, the United States invested heavily in the reconstruction of Europe's war-torn economies. It also began to rearm. The end of World War II constituted but a prelude to the subsequent Cold War.

While centered in Europe, the tensions generated by the great power rivalry spread throughout the world. In Malaysia, Indonesia, Vietnam, and the Philippines, Communist parties sought to emulate the success of their counterpart in China by toppling the governments of their nations. Working through student groups, labor unions, and cultural associations, the Soviet Union supported these movements and fortified aspiring revolutionaries in South Asia, the Middle East, and Africa as well. And when, in the late 1950s, Cuba aligned with the Soviet Union, it then provided a political base for the expansion of Soviet influence in the Western Hemisphere, thus penetrating the regional defenses of the United States.

In their struggle for global ascendancy, both the United States and Soviet Union recruited allies abroad. Each confederate, in turn, extracted a price. Fidel Castro gained from Moscow subventions to his budget and his military and access to low-cost oil. The government of Egypt received Soviet assistance in the construction of the Aswan Dam; Somalia's government, a new harbor. And governments throughout Latin America gained from the United States aid for both their civilian bureaucracies and their military establishments, increased private investment, and guaranteed prices for exports of coffee, the principal cash crop of the region.

The subsequent victory of the United States did not come on the field of battle; the United States never brought its forces directly to bear on those of the Soviet Union. Rather, the United States built a larger navy, adding new carriers, cruisers, and submarines. It recruited a larger army, and rendered it more mobile. And it procured new weapons for its air force, based upon new technologies. Realizing that their economy limited their capacity to equip their armed forces similarly, those in charge of state security in the Soviet Union backed the rise of a reformer, Mikhail Gorbachev. To renovate the economy, Gorbachev attempted to reform the polity, unleashing forces that led to the collapse of the political system—and to the end of the Cold War.

The developing nations emerged on the global stage at the beginning of the Cold War. Toward the end of the century, the Cold War abruptly ended. I shall argue that the shock unleashed by the collapse of the Soviet Union compounded the forces unleashed by the debt crisis, leading to changes in economic policy and to the restructuring of politics in the developing world.

THE LIBERALIZATION OF
ECONOMIC POLICY

At the height of the debt crisis, most developing nations could no longer borrow from private lenders. And yet they needed to be able to finance further imports and to repay past debts. International financial institutions provided emergency credits; and by working with private bankers, these institutions helped as well to restructure the obligations of the developing nations. Creditors required the governments of developing nations to adopt policies that would lower the demand for imports, and thus ease the burden of paying for previous purchases from abroad. Cuts in government deficits, higher rates of interest, and lower levels of public spending—these and other measures lowered the level of domestic demand and thus the demand for imports, reducing the burden of foreign payments on the one hand, while on the other sparking policy-induced recessions.

The longer-term response to the debt crisis lay not in the stabilization of the economies, however. Rather it lay in the reform of economic policies. It lay in the abandonment of industrial protection, the retreat from import-substituting industrialization, and the promotion of exports abroad.

In adopting policies of import-substituting industrialization, governments had sought to promote the great transformation. Shifting from the promotion of domestic industry to the promotion of exports meant for many a return to the export of primary products: timber, sugar, fruits, fibers, coffee, and others. For many developing nations, agriculture represented the past. It represented the point from which development was to begin.

The case of Brazil offers a useful example. Brazil has long

been the world's leading producer of coffee. Following World War II, Brazil launched a vigorous problem of import-substituting development. Through the Institute of Coffee, the government exploited Brazil's position in the world coffee market. Limiting exports so as to increase prices and extract revenues from foreign consumers, the institute gained fame as a skilled manager of the leading sector of Brazil's economy and became a symbol of the state's role in promoting economic development. The government devoted some of the revenues generated by the institute to the creation of infrastructure: ports, harbors, bridges, and roads. Some it on-lent to firms at subsidized rates of interest, so that they might import plant and machinery. And some it devoted to the provision of energy, building hydroelectric projects and subsidizing the costs of imported oil. Taxing agriculture on the one hand, the government promoted the creation of industry on the other, and thus pursued its goal of industrial development.

Brazil's industrial base rapidly expanded. Once lined with farms and estates, the road between Rio de Janeiro and São Paulo now ran by industrial parks and the headquarters of large corporations. But when the oil price shocks hit the economy, they revealed that the physically imposing pattern of economic growth in Brazil rested on precarious financial foundations. The government's policies had produced what became known as "the Brazilian miracle," with annual growth rates of 7 to 10 percent in the late 1960s. The government's strategy required imports of capital for the formation of industry; but by heavily taxing agriculture exports, it eroded incentives to earn foreign exchange. Brazil therefore ran high deficits abroad. And, lacking domestic sources of petroleum, the government was particularly hard hit by the subsequent rise in oil prices; Brazil had to import much of its energy. Having rapidly become an industrial giant, with its policy-induced deficits of foreign exchange and the increased costs of oil, in the 1970s Brazil become a massive debtor.

A secession of governments sought to stabilize Brazil's economy. Reducing government deficits and constricting the supply of credit, they sought to reduce the demand for imports and ease the burden of payments abroad. While the United States remained attentive to the fate of Brazil, it was also concerned with the security of its banks, many of which held Brazilian debt. With each passing year, moreover, Brazil appeared to the United States less like a needful developing nation and more like a muscular rival in international markets. With the collapse of the Soviet Union, fear of communism played less of a role in U.S. decisions about economic policy. The U.S. government therefore added its voice to those of the international financial institutions and backed their attempts to alter the policies of the government of Brazil so that it could repay its creditors.

Increasingly, the government of Brazil reduced its bias toward industry. It cut back on its credits to firms, raised its charges for loans, and reduced its subsidies for power and energy. The government also reduced its bias against agricultural exports. It abandoned its controls over the coffee market; private farms and firms were now free to sell directly to foreign companies. It stopped seizing the earnings from coffee exports for transfers to the coffers of the state. And in a gesture whose symbolism was widely heralded in Brazil, the government abolished the Institute of Coffee—the bureaucracy that had once been considered a progressive symbol of state-led growth and which had made possible the taxation of agriculture for the sake of industrial development.

THE MOVEMENT
TOWARD DEMOCRACY

Not only policy but also political systems altered in the late twentieth century. In some nations, dictators stepped aside; in others, they were overthrown. Where elections had once been mere plebiscites, they now were contested by rival parties. Many have written of the reform of policies as if they were independent of the turn to democratic forms of government. They were in fact deeply joined.

One source of linkage lies in the international financial agencies that championed the reform of policies in an effort to cope with the debt crisis. Governments constitute the shareholders of the international financial institutions and fill the seats in the boards of directors. The advanced industrial democracies contribute the bulk of capital that these agencies on-lend; as the number of votes cast by a board member is proportional to the amount of capital paid in by her government, the advanced industrial democracies therefore dominate these agencies politically as well.

Since the end of World War II, the advanced industrial nations, led by the United States, had fought to defeat communism. The toppling of the Berlin Wall and the breakup of the Soviet Union marked their victory. This radical change in the global political system helped to empower the forces of political reform in the developing world. Both domestic reformers and international do-gooders could now credibly underscore the dangers of continued authoritarianism. With the collapse of communism, the advanced industrial nations sought to consolidate the victory of democracy by securing the prosperity of the formerly Communist states. In the face of competing demands for development assistance from the former Communist bloc, the reformers could now stress that appeals for continued foreign assistance would fail unless the developing governments also became democratic.

To retain favor in the international community, autocratic heads of state therefore gingerly set into motion political reforms, designed to retain support in the Western democracies for further international lending. Those who grudgingly reformed—Daniel arap Moi in Kenya, for example—earned the grudging support of the international community and retained their hold on office. Those who did not reform—Mobutu, for example—lost the backing of the West. The need for access to international capital thus set in motion not only the reform of economic policies but also the reform of political institutions, as elites sought to deal with the new global realities.

Thus far I have focused on the international origins of political reform. But domestic pressures also animated the process of change. In several Latin American states, military governments had presided over the economy at the time of the debt crisis. The stagnation of the economy, high rates of inflation, capital flight, and rising unemployment undermined the popularity of these regimes. Professionals, businessmen, and intellectuals increasingly called for lower public deficits, greater openness of the economy, and less protectionism, while also protesting autocratic rule, the arbitrary use of force, and military government. Economic and political demands thus blended, animating new political alliances and linking demands for market-oriented policies with demands for a return to democracy.

In response to such internal opposition, democratization provided a means by which governments could remain in office, even while dealing with the new economic realities by introducing policy reforms. In Ghana, for example, the government had regulated and taxed the export of cocoa, thus diverting the revenues generated by the production of cash crops to build industries and to finance the government. The business and labor organizations that had benefited from the government's policies continued to form its political base. When, under pressure at home and abroad, the government began to change its policies, it was then compelled, in effect, to abandon its core constituency. To survive politically, it needed to cultivate a new political base and to devise new ways of staying in power.

In the process of introducing economic policy reforms, the military government of Flight Lieutenant Jerry Rawlings introduced political reforms. After carefully organizing local political councils in rural areas, Rawlings legalized the formation of political parties. Having educated the rural voters about the advantages to them of the change in government policies, Rawlings then reintroduced competitive elections. Despite decades of attempts to build an industrial base, the urban and industrial sectors of Ghana remained small by comparison with the rural and agrarian. By securing the support of the rural majority, Rawlings was therefore able to retain office, even while severing the ties between his government and its urban constituency. The change in institutions thus accommodated the change in development policy, and provided a means by which the government could retreat from policy commitments that had become economically untenable.

The cases of South Africa and Chile reveal additional linkages between democratization and elite survival in the period of economic and political reform. For decades, it had been apparent that the African majority would seize power in South Africa, a nation long ruled by its white minority. With the collapse of the Soviet Union, no enemy of the West posed a geopolitical threat to the region; the West therefore no longer needed

South Africa's military services. Nor, following the collapse of communism, was the African National Congress, the obvious successor to the white minority government, likely to remain committed to socialist doctrines. Changes in the international environment thus changed domestic political possibilities, and bowing to the inevitable, the white minority government therefore began to orchestrate its withdrawal from power.

Having presided over a brutal political regime, the incumbents feared subsequent reprisals. The mechanism that provided them assurance was their ownership of the economy. Prior to its political departure, the white majority regime privatized key economic assets, removing them from political control and placing them in the hands of private—and therefore white—shareholders. Power may have shifted to black hands; but the minority retained its ownership over the mines, the industries, and the services that generated the wealth of South Africa. As a result of its continued ascendancy in the economic realm, the white minority possessed the power to punish the black majority were it to fail subsequently to act with the restraint that it promised while negotiating the political transition. Given the minority's possession of means of punishment, the black majority's assurances that they would not seek revenge could be believed, thus easing the process of political reform.

The transition in Chile abided by an analogous logic. The right wing had aligned with the security forces, seizing power in a violent 1973 coup and brutally repressing the socialist opposition that it had displaced from power. When the military began to retreat from the political stage, its sympathizers feared that they might constitute a political minority in democratic Chile and thus be vulnerable to retaliation for the acts of the military regime. In anticipation of their loss of power, they therefore introduced a series of economic reforms, creating an independent central bank, liberalizing capital markets, and deepening credit markets in Chile. With such economic reforms in place, the right wing then felt its political future was secure. This was because should the liberal opposition, once in power, seek to renege on its promises of political restraint, capital could quickly flee the economy, harming all Chileans. The economic reforms thus provided a means of safeguarding the future of the conservatives, who otherwise might have feared peacefully to relinquish power to the political majority—a majority whose members they had once brutalized.

Changes in the international and political environments of the developing nations thus induced changes in both economic policy and political institutions. Economic collapse undermined the legitimacy of authoritarian governments; political reform provided them means of retreat. And the economic reforms that elites introduced provided means of giving credible political assurances, thus helping authoritarian incumbents to retreat from the political stage and yield to the forces of democracy.

STATE COLLAPSE

With the end of the Cold War, advanced industrial nations no longer feared that violence in the developing world posed a threat to their security. In the absence of great power rivalries, there was little danger that they might be dragged into such conflicts. Changes in the international economy placed new fiscal limits on developing regimes; no longer presiding over fountains of privilege, their political leaders found it more difficult to seduce local warlords, enticing them to disband armed retainers and to affiliate with the center. The end of the century was therefore marked not only by the spread of democracy in the developing world but also by the spread of violence.

The case of Somalia serves to illustrate the argument.

During the initial years of the Cold War, as Ethiopia had aligned with the United States, Somalia, near reflexively, aligned with the Soviet Union. When a socialist regime came to power in Ethiopia and gained the backing of the Soviet Union, Somalia then switched its allegiance to the United States. To reward its new ally—and to keep its port out of the hands of the Soviet Union—the United States provided aid to Somalia's military, built roads and power plants, and, in a country prone to drought, filled its warehouses with food.

An interpenetrating network of clans has long dominated Somalia's politics. Each clan possesses a geographic heartland; each, its own band of fighters. The political leaders of the clans organize the defense of their territory, their people, and their people's possessions; and by brokering agreements at the national level, they seek to enhance the economic and political fortunes of kin. Throughout much of the recent history of Somalia, the clan heads pursued these objectives by seeking influential positions at the national center, whence they could influence the laws that affected the welfare of their clients and gain access to the resources of the state.

The economic shocks of the 1980s crippled the economy of Somalia; the boom in oil prices, which raised the costs of domestic industry, was followed by a subsequent decline, which led to fewer remittances home from Somalis employed in the oil-producing states. The subsequent end of the Cold War led to the end of Soviet aid to Ethiopia and to a concomitant reduction in United States assistance to Somalia. As the Somali government then possessed fewer revenues, it was less able to distribute the largesse so coveted by ethnic elites. When drought subsequently returned to the region, the warlords used the military power of the clans to forage for food, first breaking into the stores amassed in public warehouses and then invading the farmlands of grain-growing regions in the south. Lacking resources, the center could not hold. Fighting among the clans fragmented the Somali state.

When the central government no longer constituted a fountain of privilege, it could no longer make it in the interests of militarized kin and communities to refrain from violence. Changes at the global level thus led to the unbinding of the bonds that had underpinned the domestic peace. Somalia joined the rapidly growing ranks of the failed states and development tragedies that marked the end of the century.

If Somalia illustrates the impact of financial stringency, then Congo (once Zaire) highlights the impact of changes in the foreign policies of the industrial nations. In the 1960s, at the height of the Cold War, the Congo had been riven with conflict. The Soviet Union backed political forces in the east of the nation; the United States, the forces of the central government. Neither wanted to run the risk of fighting, and they therefore backed intervention by international peacekeepers, employing the United Nations to put an end to the violence and to preserve the integrity of this fragile nation. In the 1990s, conflict once again broke out in Congo. But in contrast to what had once occurred, the international community now paid little attention. The Cold War was over. No longer needing a loyal henchman in the region, the United States had already abandoned its erstwhile ally, Mobutu Sese Seko. And no longer fearing Soviet expansion, the United States failed to press the international community once again to restore the integrity of this African state. Congo, which had previously been defended by the international community, now lies split asunder, its internal wars of little relevance to those with the resources with which to terminate them.

In the context of the Cold War, nations were treated as sovereign that lacked effective states. The economic shocks of the late twentieth century and the collapse of communism removed the props that had underpinned political order in the fictive states of the developing world.

THE DEVELOPING NATIONS HAD EMERGED in a bipolar world, dominated by the United States and the Soviet Union. While indeed a dangerous world, it nonetheless provided profitable and secure niches for aspirant political elites, sheltering them from military threats and providing them access to abundant support from abroad. Aggressively championing plans for rapid economic development, political elites in the developing world used their control over the economy to organize the polity, distributing patronage in order to stay in power.

With the debt crisis and the end of the Cold War, the terms for incorporation into the global community changed, and with them the politics of the developing world. The global environment became less accommodating and more dangerous. With the debt crisis of the 1980s, governments in the developing world had to curtail their level of spending. Not only did governments have to alter their economic policies; they also had to alter their political practices. The politics of patronage gave way to democracy, on the one hand, and, on the other, to political violence.

6

CONCLUSION

Then sheathes . . . in calm repose the vengeful blade,
For gentle peace in Freedom's hollowed shade.
—JOHN QUINCY ADAMS, *ALBUM*, 1842

THE STUDY OF THE POLITICAL ECONOMY of development
is the study of prosperity and violence.

Economic development occurs when persons form capital
and invest, making present sacrifices in order to reap future
gains. It occurs when they form economic organizations that
productively combine in complementary arrangements, such
that the product of the "whole"—be it a city or a firm—exceeds
the sum of what can be produced by its parts. When people
invest and combine, the city then displaces the village, the firm
displaces the farm, urban-based industry forms the core of the
economy, and prosperous societies emerge from the great transformation.

Political development occurs when people domesticate violence, transforming coercion from a means of predation into a

productive resource. Coercion becomes productive when it is employed not to seize or to destroy wealth, but rather to safeguard and promote its creation.

The political roots of development productively join with the economic when specialists in violence realize that they can best survive and prevail by promoting the prosperity of their economic base. Under such circumstances, owners of capital will believe their promises to refrain from predation. Knowing that predation would be politically unproductive, they will be willing to invest. In such circumstances, those with power will also be willing to delegate authority to those with resources and skills, enabling them to combine and to organize and, literally, to govern economic organizations. When their ability to survive, politically, depends upon the capacity of others to produce, economically, then specialists in violence will vest their power in those who will invest their capital.

In elaborating upon these themes, I have explored materials from history and from the contemporary developing world. Differences in the use of violence mark differences in the development experiences of nations in the two eras. In medieval and early modern Europe, those who governed were specialists in violence; the job of the state was war. In the modern period, the global environment checked the tendency to fight. In so doing, it separated the need to arm, and thus to survive, from the need to enhance the wealth of the nation. It therefore modified the trajectory that had once characterized the process of development.

Exceptions to the rule often prove informative, and I therefore return to the case of Brazil. Brazil was the only nation in Latin America that sent its military to fight in World War II. Its army joined that of the United States in Italy, where its troops experienced the realities of modern warfare. Upon their return home, Brazilian officers were appalled by the inability of civilian politicians to comprehend the gap between the demands of modern war and the capacity of their country to meet them. Without a massive increase in the industrial capacity of Brazil, they realized, they could never safeguard their state should another country seek to impose its will. Focusing on the vision of lavish abundance and profligate destruction that they had witnessed in combat, when they later took power, the officers impatiently drove Brazil along the path to industrial development, accelerating the Brazilian miracle— and laying the foundations for its subsequent crisis of debt.

Other developing nations have also encountered the realities of modern war. Turkey did so in World War I. In World War II, so too did the nations of the Pacific Rim: Japan, Korea, China, and Taiwan. In such nations, governments learned to treat the national economy as a military resource, to be nurtured and fed rather than plundered. Targeting projects and sectors whose progress they deemed essential to security—the creation of a shipyard, for example, or the development of a chemical industry—warriors and bureaucrats sought investments from capitalists and businessmen. Recognizing the imperative driving those in charge of policy, those with capital calculated that their governments were sincere in wishing that their ventures succeed, and so invested. Those in charge of the state also recognized the necessity of investing their power, delegating its use to entrepreneurs and businessmen and permitting them to organize. By safeguarding firms and investments, and by placing the power of the state in the hands of those who would use it to form economic organizations, those who oversaw the use of violence sought to lay the economic foundations for military security in the nations of the Pacific Rim.

Elsewhere, the state system that prevailed after World War II provided sufficient safeguards that political elites did not tend to treat economic policy-making as a matter of political survival. The strategic setting in which they operated did little to render credible their assurances to those with capital; nor were they driven, as a matter of state security, to place their power in private hands, enabling those with wealth to structure means to govern the organization of economic activity. Lacking the spur of the risk of survival, in most developing countries, those with power confronted few incentives to render coercion economically productive.

Differences in the structure of power at the global level have thus produced differences in the use of violence at the national level. Variations in the incentives faced internationally thus help to account for differences in the behavior of states over time and, within the modern era, over place.

EXTENSIONS AND IMPLICATIONS

Capital provides one source of growth; the organization of economic activities provides another. In conclusion, I seek to deepen our understanding of the political economy of development by exploring more closely the use of power to defend, or to fail to defend, the accumulation of capital and the formation of economic organizations.

ACCUMULATION

I begin with a case—that of the cocoa industry in Ghana. As incomes rose in the advanced industrial nations of Europe, people consumed greater amounts of chocolate, which they prized for its flavor and for the stimulation it provided when consumed as a beverage. Merchants rounded the cape of West Africa, entered its harbors, and placed a growing volume of orders for the beans from which chocolate is made. And people from the coastal cities of West Africa moved inland to establish cocoa farms in the tropical forests of the region.

So dense was the undergrowth of the West African forest that scores of workers had to be hired and kept on for seasons in order to clear and establish a cocoa farm. Investors had to construct roads, bridge ravines, and lay pontoons over rivers before they could evacuate the product from the forest and transport it to coastal ports. The seedlings, moreover, required years of growth before yielding a crop. The development of the cocoa industry therefore required large amounts of capital.

In a fascinating study of the political dimensions of this transformation, Kathryn Firmin-Sellers (1996) traces the history of Akyem Abuakwa, an indigenous state in the forest of what is now Ghana. She focuses in particular on one Nana Ofori Atta, the respected and wily paramount chief of Akyem Abuakwa in the early years of the rise of the cocoa industry. Aware that investors would withhold their capital unless assured of property rights, Nana Ofori Atta sought to strengthen the power of his chiefdom so as to defend the rights of investors. But Ofori Atta was also aware of what Barry Weingast (1995, 1) has called "the fundamental political dilemma of an economic system"—that "a government strong enough to protect property rights . . . is also strong enough to confiscate the wealth of its citizens."

To address this problem, while seeking to enhance his executive powers, Nana Ofori Atta also sought to place visible and credible limits on his political discretion. He introduced reforms in the government of the "tribe" such that he, the chief, became accountable, both politically and financially, to a council behooven to private civilians. The council approved all taxes. It could depose the chief. It paid him. And it paid the salaries of the administrators and police whom the chief superintended. Given the structure that Nana Ofori Atta devised, Firmin-Sellers argues, it became clear that the chief could not use his power to prey upon the private sector; if he desired greater revenues for his government, he would have to use his powers to promote the creation of private wealth. Indeed, Firmin-Sellers stresses, investment appears to have boomed, as Nana Ofori Atta had intended. By placing his financial and political fortunes in the hands of a civilian council, Nana Ofori Atta appears successfully to have signaled that he would use his powers to advance the interests of those who created, and enjoyed, the wealth of the cocoa industry.

As we have seen, the tale told by Firmin-Sellers finds its parallel in history. The creation of parliamentary forms of government creates incentives for those who possess power to employ it in the interests of those who possess wealth. It provides assurances to those with capital that, should they invest— and so increase the wealth of the nation—those who control the instruments of coercion will refrain from appropriating the value that they generate.

In exploring the differences between governments in rich and poor nations, it is useful, once again, to return to the history of Akyem Abuakwa. Under the stewardship of Nana Ofori Atta, the kingdom prospered. But with the coming of independence, Kwame Nkrumah, the first president of Ghana, sought to promote the industrial development of the nation. To secure the capital by which to finance his plans, Nkrumah imposed a government monopoly on the export of cocoa and high levels of taxation on the earnings of cocoa farmers. The forest kingdoms, including Akyem Abuakwa, organized in opposition to Nkrumah's policies. In response, the government destroyed the political power of those kingdoms, branding their governments as "tribal" and therefore as a threat to the future of the nation. The policies pursued by Nkrumah's government and, indeed, by most that followed led to a withdrawal of capital from farming, to a decline in the production of cash crops, and to the impoverishment of Ghana.

The creation of limited government may not be sufficient to secure high levels of investment, much less the growth of national economies. But assurances to investors surely are necessary to secure the formation of capital. Too often, in the developing world, politicians fail to induce the selection of policies that offer attractive prospects to investors. And institutions too rarely impose limits upon those who would use power to prey upon the wealth of others. The use of coercion for predation is too little checked; its use to promote the creation of wealth is too weakly motivated. Political risk therefore clouds the prospects offered to those with capital, thus hindering investment and retarding the development of nations.[1]

ORGANIZATION

Economic development results not merely from the formation of capital but also from the creation of organizations. In particular, it results when the state confers upon private citizens the

---

[1] In connection with this argument, it is useful to contrast the conduct of governments in resource-rich nations with that of governments in nations less favorably endowed . In both, governments search for revenues; but they do so in different ways. Those in resource-rich economies tend to secure revenues by extracting them; those in resource-poor nations, by promoting the creation of wealth. Differences in natural endowments thus appear to shape the behavior of governments. While other factors clearly pertain, this argument may shed light on differences between the conduct of governments in, say, resource-poor Asia, which appear willing to safeguard the creation of wealth and to promote the creation of powerful private economic organizations, and the conduct of governments in, say, resource-rich Africa, which often behave in a predatory manner.

authority to reward, or to penalize, others, thereby making it in their private interests to behave in ways that enhance the collective welfare. When the charter conferred by a king empowers a citizen of a city to compel those who benefit from the construction of a wharf, the deepening of a river, or the building of a bridge to share in the costs of its construction, then the government unleashes incentives that generate the creation of wealth and promotes the development of the economy. And when a manager can impose costs upon one division of a firm—as by compelling it to speed its production, or to change its product line—such that other units might benefit, to the advantage of the larger enterprise, then the governance structure of that firm itself becomes a source of value, enhancing the worth of the enterprise. The orchestration of complementarities, the building of teams, and the organization of productive enterprises require that economic agents possess the authority to govern.

Coercion, once tamed, can thus be productive.[2] While its delegation by the state does produce economic benefits, it can also impose costs. And to induce development, these costs must be minimized.

Collusion   With the power to organize, private agents can increase their earnings. They can do so by organizing efficient means of production, increasing total output, and thereby contributing to the growth of the economy; alternatively, they can do so by colluding, limiting production, and forcing up prices, thereby enriching themselves at the expense of others. The

---

[2] Just below the surface of this argument lurks a critique of the now fashionable literature on "social capital" (see Putnam 1993). While those who extol the power of social capital look to society as the source of productivity, I instead look to the state, and see the existence of the private capacity for governance as resulting from the choices made by those with political power.

capacity to organize can thus result not only in productive organization but also in collusion, whose primary beneficiaries may become rich, but only because they have lowered the incomes of others.

The capacity to organize may thus be a necessary condition for economic growth, but clearly it is not sufficient. Among other necessary factors, it would appear, is the spur of competition. We know that large, complex, and highly organized firms dominate the industrial base of Sweden, Switzerland, and other small industrial economies. But because the governments of these nations keep their markets open, these firms must compete against others located in other nations; they cannot convert their large size into market power. And we know that when markets are large, they may remain competitive, even though containing large firms. It may in fact take several large firms, each operating efficiently, to satisfy demand in the market, meaning that in nations such as the United States, large firms may confront large competitors.

Not only economic competition but also political competition plays a role in shaping the use of power by economic agents. Under central planning, the economies of the Communist nations of Eastern Europe and the former Soviet Union had been dominated by a small number of large enterprises; and with the transition to private ownership, managers, bureaucrats, and well-placed politicians had gained control of these firms. In a recent study, Joel Hellman (1998) notes that the new owners formed organizations that attempted to restrict market competition and pressure groups that lobbied for government bailouts. What distinguished successful transitions from those that stalled, Hellman argues, was the degree to which these short-term winners faced political competition from those who would have been harmed by their efforts to collude. When political parties competed for power in these transition economies, politicians possessed incentives to champion the interests of the many, who stood to loose from the political efforts of the privileged few. Rather than letting the short-term winners adopt policies that caused the reforms to stall, by appealing to the power of the broader electorate, political challengers forced the government to press on with economic reforms and to reaffirm market-oriented policies. Hellman thus suggests that political contestability, as well as market competition, shapes the way in which power is employed by private agents.[3]

While the delegation of public power to economic agents may energize growth, then, it also poses significant dangers. Just as military captains once employed their power to seize wealth through battle, so too can captains of industry employ their power to secure redistributive gains in the marketplace. When public power is delegated to economic agents, it must be conferred upon those who face competition for it to be used productively.

Redistributive Politics   Not only firms but also communities can constitute productive forms of economic organization. Already noted is the manner in which the elites of Akyem

---

[3] A similar argument could be made for the United States, where popular—indeed, populist—opposition to the power of cartels led to the passage of the Sherman Antitrust Act. A key question in comparative political economy thus becomes: Under what conditions does the desire to limit the use of economic power produce legislation designed to promote market competition, as opposed to legislation that would publicly regulate it, as by nationalizing large firms?

Also relevant is the comparative analysis of the coffee industries in East Africa and Colombia. Single-party systems dominated the nations of the first, while in Colombia political parties competed for control of the government. The single-party regimes of East Africa stifled the creation of wealth-creating economic organizations in the coffee sector, whereas the government of Colombia vested public powers in an organization that enhanced the profitability of coffee production. See Bates (1997).

Abuakwa restructured public power so as to secure investments in the forest economy of inland Ghana. To this account could be added others. Local communities throughout the developing world impose taxes upon themselves, in terms of money and labor; organize; and invest in the construction of water supplies, market centers, and schools. Through such actions, community activists, cultural leaders, and ethnic organizations lay clam to space in the political structures of the developing nations and contribute to the growth of their economies.

Such groups supply needed services, create valuable infrastructure, and promote the improvement of public infrastructure. Using their powers, they promote economic development. But the power they possess not only can be employed to create value. It can also be employed to destroy.

Recall the discussion of lineages and kinship groups with which this book began. As each increases in size numerically it also increases in size geographically as its households segment, migrate, and occupy new territories. With the growth and spread of kin and communities, groups come to contest the positions of others, laying claim to land, water supplies, grazing rights, and markets. As the Kikuyu spread down and out from Mount Kenya, for example, they entered the lands of others and initiated a protracted process of negotiating, and fighting, over contested terrain. When local communities employ their capacity to organize, they may not only launch valuable projects, but also campaigns to lay claim to the resources possessed by others.

One outcome may be violence. In the rich highlands of East Africa, the diamond fields of Sierra Leone, and the river basins of Colombia, rural communities have taken up arms and the battles they fight disrupt the national political order. Less dramatically—although of equal significance, perhaps—competition among such communities weaken the incentives that constrain the behavior of governments. When communities compete among themselves, governments—even those that are electorally chosen—can slip the bonds of accountability.

To grasp the point, return to the case of Ghana. Nkrumah was able to seize the wealth of Akyem Abuakwa and other cocoa-exporting chiefdoms when he gained the backing of poorer groups, to whom he promised to transfer that wealth in the form of government projects. What was true in Ghana is valid more generally. When a government can retain power by forming coalitions among ethnic communities, and when it can use that power to seize revenues from those outside this core constituency, then no group can afford to withhold its political support, for fear of becoming the object of political predation. Redistributive local rivalries can produce a pattern of politics in which citizens compete to back the government in power, thus freeing it from the restraints normally associated with political accountability. The benefits created by the organized efforts of such groups at the local level may thus be outweighed by the losses they induce at the national level, since they provide a political environment in which unproductive governments can remain in power. Competition among communal groups might appear as a sign of vigorous civic life. It may also constitute a political pathology because it may enable governments to remain in office while using their power not to create wealth, but to capture and redistribute it.

The case of Uganda helps to illustrate this argument. In many ways, Uganda resembles Ghana. While not bordering an ocean, Uganda nonetheless possesses a long shoreline, with towns and cities lying along the coast of Lake Victoria. Like Ghana, it possesses an impoverished north, where families subsist by herding cattle and growing sorghum and millet. And it possesses as well a prosperous forest zone, from which most of its wealth flows from the production of cash crops. As was the case in Ghana, following independence in Uganda, a socialist politician took power. Like Nkrumah, Prime Minister Milton Obote played the poor communities off against the rich, seizing the wealth of those who had invested in the creation of coffee farms in the forest in order to secure the revenues for industry and for the financing of projects that would benefit the poorer communities. Pitting one group and one region against others, Obote held on to power, even while pursuing policies that impoverished his nation.

THE FATE OF UGANDA, like that of Ghana, thus illustrates how governments can exploit the rivalry among local communities and survive, politically, even while failing to generate economic growth. But Uganda also provides evidence of a second major danger. Those political leaders who helped to organize ethnic political communities in Uganda also succeeded in arming them, transforming them into militarized movements.

It was these forces that I had encountered in Bugisu, the coffee-growing district on the slopes of Mount Elgon. It was these forces too that had terrorized the colleagues with whom I worked, demoralizing them as parents and professionals and plunging them into grief for those killed by marauding soldiers.

I returned several times to Uganda, the last as a member of a team dispatched by the World Bank to advise and assist in the reconstruction of its war-torn economy. Upon my departure, I sought a framework within which to grasp what I had experienced there. And I still recall the palpable shock I felt when reading the paragraph by Hobbes that concludes "and the life of man,

TABLE 6.1

*Terms of World Bank Mission to Uganda, 1982,
and Thomas Hobbes,* Leviathan, *1*

THE WORLD BANK The Mission shall advise on measures to:	THOMAS HOBBES
Promote industrial development;	"there is no place for industry, because the fruit thereof is uncertain;
Promote agricultural production;	"and consequently no culture of the earth;
Promote foreign trade;	"no navigation, nor use of the commodities that may be imported by sea;
Accelerate physical reconstruction;	"no commodious buildings; no instruments of moving, and removing, such things as require much force;
Strengthen and revitalize the research and education system, in agriculture and more generally;	"no knowledge of the face of the earth; no account of time; no arts; no letters;
Secure political order.	no society; and what is worst of all, continual fear, and danger of violent death; and the life of man, solitary, poor, nasty, brutish, and short."

Source: "Terms of World Bank, Structural Adjustment Mission to Uganda, 1982."
Thomas Hobbes, 1651, *Leviathan,* in William Ebenstein, *Great Political Thinkers*,
3rd ed. (New York: Holt, Rinehart and Winston, 1961), p. 368.

solitary, poor, nasty, brutish, and short." For clause by clause, the desolate lines in that paragraph echo the terms of the mission that had been sent out to promote development in the nation (see Table 6.1).

Hobbes wrote in reaction to events that occurred long ago. But his words disturb because they respond to much that is felt and seen in the present day, when, for too many in the developing world, insecurity remains the norm and development a dream that cruelly eludes their grasp.

Central to development is the passage of time. In Uganda, the future was uncertain. Less dramatically, perhaps, it has been in other developing counties as well. Control over the means of violence remains in the hands of private parties; kin, community, and political rivals have yet to be disarmed. In such circumstances, much that is elevated cannot be attained; much that is desirable cannot be secured. By addressing the relationship between prosperity and violence, this book has investigated the political foundations of development.

NOTES FOR FURTHER READING

1. INTRODUCTION

The classical treatments of development as the process of structural change remain those of Kuznets (1966) and Chenery and Taylor (1968). Polanyi (1944) advances a similar argument, but in a distinctive and idiosyncratic manner. For a conventional treatment of development economics, see Gillis et al. (1987); for a "social democratic" voice, consult Todaro (1994); and for a repeatedly updated collection of papers drawn from contemporary Marxian writings, consult the various editions of Wilbur's anthology (e.g., Wilbur 1973).

Market-oriented studies of development would include Little (1982), Lal (1983), and Bauer (1954). Those taking inspiration from the state-led growth of east Asia would include Amsden (1989) and Wade (1990); see as well the World Bank study (World Bank 1993). For a critique of these arguments, see Fishlow et al. (1994); for further extensions of them, turn to Evans (1995).

For approaches utilizing the new institutionalism, see the contributions in Harriss, Hunter, and Lewis (1995) and Borner and Paldam (1998). Influential in this field, as in his own, is the work of Douglass North, an economic historian; most relevant, perhaps, is North and Thomas (1973). See also Marx (1906), Putterman (1986), Tirole (1989), and Williamson (1985). For discussions of complementarities and economies of scale, see Cornes and Sandler (1986) and Cooper (1999).

For studies of the coffee industry in East Africa, see Bates (1989 and 1997) and Bunker (1987).

2. AGRARIAN SOCIETIES

Anthropologists have written a large number of highly accessible and engaging introductory texts, among the most relevant of which number those by Wolff (1966) and Sahlins (1968). Sahlins's classic article (1961) deeply shapes this essay, as do the action-oriented approaches to social anthropology produced by Bailey (1969) and members of the "Manchester school," such as Epstein (1992), Mitchell (1956), and van Velsen (1974). See also Elizabeth Colson's classic (1974). Fortes's effort to incorporate the "temporal dimension" into the study of social structure has deeply influenced my thinking (see the review in Goody 1958). The Marxist contributions that most directly affect this work are those by Meillassoux (1984) and Godellier (1972).

Among the many studies of the Kikuyu, the most relevant to this essay is the study of expansion and migration by Leakey (1977). For further references, consult those contained in Bates (1989).

Wharton (1971) wrote a pioneering essay on the impact of risk on agrarian societies. For more contemporary contributions, see those collected by Bardhan (1989). Halstead and O'Shea

(1989) provide a fascinating alternative to the writings of economists. Scott's classic (1976) applies the analysis of risk to agrarian politics; Popkin (1979) offers an important critique.

For additional studies of village communities, see Redfield (1973), Foster (1967), Colson (1974), Scott (1976), and Scott and Kerkvliet (1986). For additional insights into feuding, see Black-Michaud (1975), Cohen (1995), Dresch (1989), and Hardy (1963).

3. THE FORMATION OF STATES

For studies of the impact of cities on agriculture, see, among others, Boserup (1981); Hoffman (1996); Woude, Hayami, and de Vries (1990); and Brenner (1976). DeLong and Shleifer (1993) offer important insights. The works of Arthur (1994) and Krugman (1991) are of course central to this argument.

For the recruitment of retainers in households, see the rich literature on so-called bastard feudalism. Pioneered by McFarlane (1973, 1981), this literature has been enriched by the works of Hicks (1995) and Duby (1991).

It was Hintze, perhaps, who pioneered the study of the domestic impact of warfare (see Gilbert 1975); Tilly (1975) and Skocpol (1979) extend this tradition (see also Trimberger 1978). The works of Downing (1992), McNeil (1982), and van Creveld (1977) remain invaluable. Heckscher (1955) and Viner (1991) explore the use of economic policy to build states; crucial as well are the classic contributions of Weber (1968) and Smith (1976). Bellot (1902), who writes on Inns of Court in London, offers a rich study of the internal life of a guild.

Margaret Levi has deeply probed the politics of resource extraction by states. For her treatment of taxation, see Levi (1988); for her treatment of recruitment, see Levi (1977). Her

"Predatory Theory of Rule" (1981) remains a classic and has greatly affected my thinking. Kennedy (1989) also addresses these issues. Central too is the work of Giddens (1987).

For discussions of the use of the public revenues to demobilize local elites, see Peck (1990) and Root (1994); see also MacCaffrey (1961), Ward (1992), Hurstfield (1958), and Waugh (1988).

For studies of food supply, see Outhwaite (1981), Ormrod (1985), Tilly (1975), and Smith (1976). The debates over economic policy during the wars between England and France are beautifully captured by Kaplan (1976); see also Meek (1963).

4. STATE FORMATION IN THE MODERN ERA

The best discussions of the structure of protection created by import-substituting industrialization appear in Lal (1983), Little, Scitovsky, and Scott (1970), and Krueger (1996). For background, see Hirschman (1958), Gerschenkron (1966), and Meier and Seers (1984). For some of the classic texts in dependency theory, consult the various editions of the reader by Wilbur (e.g., 1973).

Waltz (1979) provides the classic analysis of the bipolar structure of power in the postwar period; Jackson (1990), the definitive analysis of its impact upon state building. See also Moore (1998) and van de Walle (forthcoming).

On the impact of public finance on the behavior of states, see Levi (1981, 1988) and Goldstone (1991). Hoffman and Norberg (1994) and Rosenthal (1998) develop lines of argument that converge upon those advanced herein. Prestwich (1972), Mitchell (1951), and Willard (1934) provide some of the most illuminating materials on taxation. See also Pollard (1926). Portions of Sheppard (1998) provide valuable insight into the mobilization of public credit. Excellent material on the impact of the Dutch on British political and economic institutions appears in (Israel 1991a, b).

For Zaire, consult Winsome (1993) and Schatzberg (1988, 1991); for Indonesia, *Time* (Asia) (May 24, 1999); for Kenya, Barry (1975), Njonjo (1977), and Swainson (1979).

5. LATE-CENTURY SHOCKS TO THE GLOBAL SYSTEM

The debt crisis gave rise to a copious literature. Sachs (1989) offers a useful introduction. Stephan Haggard launched a series of comparative studies of response to the crisis, some focusing on policy-making (e.g., Haggard, Lee, and Maxfield 1993) and others on institutional reform (e.g., Haggard and Webb 1994). Mosley, Harrington, and Toye (1991) crafted a major study of the role of international institutions in this crisis.

The case of Brazil rests on Abreu (1980), Bacha (1988), Bates (1997), Frieden (1991), Lal and Maxfield (1993), Maxfield (1997), and Skidmore (1967). For materials on Ghana, see Rothchild (1991), Herbst (1993), and Leith and Lofchie (1993).

For studies of democratization, see Huntington (1991), O'Donnell and Schmitter (1986), Przeworski (1991), and Haggard and Webb (1994). See also Bates (1991).

Among the leading studies of the militarization of politics is that by Reno (1995). See also Bayart (1993). For Zaire and Somalia, see Schatzberg (1988, 1991), Winsome (1993), Zartman (1995), and Clark and Herbst (1995). For South Africa, see Greenberg (1987); for Chile, see Stallings and Brock (1993), Boylan (1999), and Londregan (2000). Grossman (1991), Fearon (1995), Collier and Hoeffler (1989), and others (e.g., Kuran 1989) are developing new analytic and empirical foundations for the study of political violence. See also Bates, Greif, and Singh (1998); Bates and LaFerrara (1999); and Wantchekon (1996).

6. CONCLUSION

For studies of the nations of the Pacific Rim, see Amsden (1989), Wade (1990), the World Bank (1993), and Evans (1995).

The theoretical arguments are influenced not only by Levi (1981, 1988) but also by Weingast (1995) and North and Weingast (1989). In addition to the readings cited in the notes on chapter 1, consult also Berle and Means (1932) and McConnell (1966).

The literature on the small open economies starts with Cameron (1978) and Katzenstein (1985). For analytic approaches to the political economy of policy reform, see Sturzenegger and Tommasi (1998). The analysis of the impact of ethnicity rests on Ferejohn (1986).

Douglas Rimmer, like myself a student of Africa, has also been struck by the relevance of Hobbes to contemporary developing nations and offers intriguing insights into the origins of the passage that we both quote. See Rimmer (1995).

BIBLIOGRAPHY

Abreu, Marcelo de Pavia, ed. 1980. *A Ordem do Progresso.* Rio de Janeiro: Editora Campus.

Amsden, Alice H. 1989. *Asia's Next Giant: South Korea and Late Industrialization.* New York: Oxford University Press.

Anonymous. 1990. *The Song of Roland.* Translated by D. D. R. Owen. Woodbridge, Eng.: Boydell Press.

Arthur, Brian. 1994. *Increasing Returns and Path Dependence in the Economy.* Ann Arbor, Mich.: University of Michigan Press.

Ausenda, Giorgio, ed. 1995. *After Empire: Towards an Ethnology of Europe's Barbarians.* Studies in Historical Archaeoethnology, vol. 1. Woodbridge, Eng. Boydell Press.

Bacha, Edmar, ed. 1988. *Os Mitos de Uma Década.* Rio de Janeiro: Paz e Terra.

Bailey, F. G. 1969. *Stratagems and Spoils.* New York: Schocken Books.

Bardhan, Pranab, ed. 1989. *The Economic Theory of Agricultural Institutions.* Oxford: Clarendon Press.

Barry, John. 1975. Kenya on the Brink. *Sunday Times* (London). August 10, 17, and 24.

Bartlett, Robert. 1993. *The Making of Europe: Conquest, Colonization, and Cultural Change, 950–1350.* Princeton, N.J.: Princeton University Press.

Bartlett, Robert, and Angus Mackay, eds. 1989. *Medieval Frontier Societies*. Oxford: Clarendon Press.

Bates, Robert H. 1983. The Preservation of Order in Stateless Societies. In *Essays on the Political Economy of Rural Africa*, edited by R. H. Bates. Berkeley and Los Angeles: University of California Press.

————. 1989. *Beyond the Miracle of the Market*. Cambridge: Cambridge University Press.

————. 1991. The Economics of the Transition to Democracy. *P. S.* 24, no. 1:24–27.

————. 1997. *Open Economy Politics*. Princeton, N.J.: Princeton University Press.

Bates, Robert H., Avner Greif, and Smita Singh. 1998. *Organizing Violence*. Cambridge Mass., and Stanford, Calif. Typescript.

Bates, Robert H., and Eliana LaFerrara. 1999. *Ethnicity, Politics, and Violence*. Cambridge, Mass. Typescript.

Bauer, P. T. 1954. *West African Trade*. Cambridge: Cambridge University Press.

Bayart, Jean-François. 1993. *The State in Africa: The Politics of the Belly*. New York: Longman.

Bellot, Hugh H. L. 1902. *The Inner and Middle Temple*. London: Methuen.

Berle, Adolph, and Gardiner Means. 1932. *The Modern Corporation and Private Property*. New York: Macmillan.

Berry, Sara. 1993. *No Condition Is Permanent*. Madison, Wisc.: University of Wisconsin Press.

Black-Michaud, Jacob. 1975. *Cohesive Force: Feud in the Mediterranean and Middle East*. Oxford: Blackwell.

Blum, Jerome. 1961. *Lord and Peasant in Russia*. Princeton, N.J.: Princeton University Press.

Bohannan, Paul. 1989. *Justice and Judgment among the Tiv*. Prospect Heights, Ill.: Waveland Press.

Bohannan, Paul, and George Dalton, eds. 1962. *Markets in Africa*. Evanston, Ill.: Northwestern University Press.

Borner, Silvio, and Martin Paldam, eds. 1998. *The Political Dimension of Economic Growth*. New York: St. Martin's Press.

Boserup, Ester. 1965. *The Conditions of Agricultural Growth*. London: Allen and Unwin.

————. 1981. *Population and Technological Change*. Chicago: University of Chicago Press.

Boylan, Delia. 1999. *The Politics of Economic Policy Reform*. Typescript.

Brenner, Robert. 1976. Agrarian Class Structure and Economic Development in Pre-Industrial Europe. *Past and Present* 70 (February): 30–75.

————. 1993. *Merchants and Revolution: Commercial Change, Political Conflict, and London's Overseas Traders, 1550–1653*. Princeton, N.J.: Princeton University Press.

Bunker, Stephen G. 1987. *Peasants Against the State*. Urbana, Ill.: University of Illinois Press.

Byock, Jesse L. 1982. *Feud in Icelandic Saga*. Berkeley and Los Angeles: University of California Press.

Cameron, David. 1978. The Expansion of the Public Economy. *American Political Science Review* 72 (December): 1243–61.

Carneiro, Robert L. 1970. A Theory of the Origin of the State. *Science* 169, no. 3946:733–38.

Chenery, Hollis B., and Lance J. Taylor. 1968. Development Patterns: Among Countries and over Time. *Review of Economics and Statistics* 50 (November): 391–416.

Clark, Walter, and Jeffrey Herbst. 1995. *Somalia and the Future of Humanitarian Intervention*. Princeton, N.J.: Center of International Studies, Princeton University.

Cohen, David. 1995. *Law, Violence, and Community in Classical Athens*. Cambridge: Cambridge University Press.

Collier, Paul, and Anke Hoeffler. 1989. On Economic Causes of Civil War. *Oxford Economic Papers* 50:563–73.

Colson, Elizabeth. 1974. *Tradition and Contract*. Chicago: Aldine.

Cooper, Russell W. 1999. *Coordination Games*. Cambridge: Cambridge University Press.

Cornes, Richard, and Todd Sandler. 1986. *The Theory of Externalities, Public Goods, and Club Goods*. Cambridge: Cambridge University Press.

deLong, J. Bradford, and Andrei Shleifer. 1993. Princes and Merchants. *Journal of Law and Economics* 36 (October): 671–702.

Dixit, Avinash K., and Robert S. Pindyck. 1994. *Investment under Uncertainty*. Princeton, N.J.: Princeton University Press.

Downing, Brian M. 1992. *The Military Revolution and Political Change.* Princeton: Princeton University Press.

Dresch, Paul. 1989. *Tribes, Government, and History in Yemen.* Oxford: Oxford University Press.

Duby, Georges. 1991. *France in the Middle Ages, 987–1460.* Translated by Juliet Vale. Oxford: Blackwell.

Epstein, A. L. 1992. *Scenes from African Urban Life.* Edinburgh: Edinburgh University Press.

Evans, Peter. 1995. *Embedded Autonomy: States and Industrial Transformation.* Princeton, N.J.: Princeton University Press.

Evans-Pritchard, E. E. 1940. *The Nuer.* Oxford: Clarendon Press.

Fearon, James. 1995. Rationalist Explanations for War. *International Organizations* 49, no. 3:379–414.

Ferejohn, John. 1986. Incumbent Performance and Electoral Control. *Public Choice* 50:5–25.

Firmin-Sellers, Kathryn. 1995. The Politics of Property Rights. *American Political Science Review* 89, no. 4:867–82.

———. 1996. *The Transformation of Property Rights in the Gold Coast.* Cambridge: Cambridge University Press.

Fishlow, Albert, Catherine Gwin, Stepan Haggard, Dani Rodrik, and Robert Wade. 1994. *Miracle or Design? Lessons from the East Asian Experience.* Washington, D.C.: Overseas Development Council.

Foster, George. 1967. *Tzintzuntzan.* Boston: Little Brown.

Frieden, Jeffry A. 1991. *Debt, Development and Democracy.* Princeton, N.J.: Princeton University Press.

Gerschenkron, Alexander. 1966. *Economic Backwardness in Historical Perspective.* Cambridge, Mass.: Belknap Press of Harvard University Press.

Giddens, Anthony. 1987. *The Nation-States and Violence.* Berkeley and Los Angeles: University of California Press.

Gilbert, Felix, ed. 1975. *The Historical Essays of Otto Hintze.* New York: Oxford University Press.

Gillis, Malcolm, Dwight H. Perkins, Michael Roemer, and Donald R. Snodgrass. 1987. *Economics of Development.* New York: W. W. Norton.

Gluckman, Max. 1955. *Custom and Conflict in Africa.* Oxford: Blackwell.

Godelier, Maurice. 1972. *Rationality and Irrationality in Economics.* New York: Monthly Review Press.

Goldstone, Jack A. 1991. *Revolution and Rebellion in the Early Modern World.* Berkeley and Los Angeles: University of California Press.

Goody, Jack, ed. 1958. *The Developmental Cycle in Domestic Groups.* Cambridge: Cambridge University Press.

Greenberg, Stanley. 1987. *Legitimating the Illegitimate.* Berkeley and Los Angeles: University of California Press.

Grossman, Herschel I. 1991. A General Equilibrium Model of Insurrections. *American Economic Review* 81, no. 4:912–21.

Haggard, Stephan, Chung H. Lee, and Sylvia Maxfield, eds. 1993. *The Politics of Finance in Developing Countries.* Ithaca, N.Y.: Cornell University Press.

Haggard, Stephan, and Steven B. Webb, eds. 1994. *Voting for Reform.* New York: World Bank Oxford University Press.

Halstead, Paul, and John O'Shea, eds. 1989. *Bad Year Economics.* Cambridge: Cambridge University Press.

Hardy, M. J. L. 1963. *Blood Feuds and the Payment of Blood Money in the Middle East.* Beirut: Catholic Press.

Harriss, John, Janet Hunter, and Colin M. Lewis, eds. 1995. *The New Institutional Economics and Third World Development.* London and New York: Routledge.

Hechter, Michael, and William Brustein. 1980. Regional Modes of Production and Patterns of State Formation in Western Europe. *American Journal of Sociology* 85, no. 5:1061–94.

Heckscher, Eli F. 1955. *Mercantilism.* 2 vols. New York and London: Allen and Unwin.

Hellman, Joel S. 1998. Winners Take All: The Politics of Partial Reform in Postcommunist Transitions. *World Politics.* 50, no. 2:203–34.

Henneman, J. B. 1971. *Royal Taxation in Fourteenth Century France.* Princeton, N.J.: Princeton University Press.

Herbst, Jeffrey. 1993. *The Politics of Reform in Ghana.* Berkeley and Los Angeles: University of California Press.

Hicks, Michael. 1995. *Bastard Feudalism.* New York and London: Longman.

Hirschman, Albert O. 1958. *The Strategy of Economic Development.* New Haven: Yale University Press.

————. 1977. *The Passions and the Interests.* Princeton, N.J.: Princeton University Press.

Hoffman, Philip T. 1996. *Growth in a Traditional Society: The French Countryside, 1450–1815.* Princeton, N.J.: Princeton University Press.

Hoffman, Philip, and Kathryn Norberg, eds. 1994. *Fiscal Crisis, Liberty and Representative Government.* Stanford, Calif.: Stanford University Press.

Hudson, John. 1996. *The Formation of the English Common Law.* New York and London: Longman.

Huntington, Samuel P. 1991. *The Third Wave.* Norman, Okla.: University of Oklahoma Press.

Hurstfield, Joel. 1958. *The Queen's Wards.* London: Longmans, Green and Company.

————. 1961. The Succession Struggle in Late Elizabethan England. In *Elizabethan Government and Society*, edited by S. T. Bindhoff, J. Hurstfield, and C. H. Williams. London: University of London at the Athlone Press.

Israel, Jonathan. 1991a. The Dutch Role in the Glorious Revolution. In *The Anglo-Dutch Moment*, edited by J. Israel. Cambridge: Cambridge University Press.

————. 1991b. General Introduction. In *The Anglo-Dutch Moment*, edited by J. Israel. Cambridge: Cambridge University Press.

Jackson, Robert H. 1990. *Quasi-States: Sovereignty, International Relations, and the Third World.* New York: Cambridge University Press.

Kaplan, Steven L. 1976. *Bread, Politics, and Political Economy in the Reign of Louis XV.* The Hague: Martin Nijhoff.

Katzenstein, Peter. 1985. *Small States in World Markets.* Ithaca, N.Y.: Cornell University Press.

Kennedy, Paul. 1989. *The Rise and Fall of the Great Powers: Economic Change and Military Conflict from 1500 to 2000.* New York: Vintage.

Klein, Benjamin, Robert Crawford, and Armen Alchien. 1978. Vertical Integration, Appropriable Rents, and the Competitive Contracting Process. *Journal of Law and Economics* 21:297–326.

Krueger, Anne O., ed. 1996. *The Political Economy of Trade Protection.* Chicago: University of Chicago Press.

Krugman, Paul. 1991. *Geography and Trade*. Cambridge, Mass.: MIT Press.

Kuran, Timur. 1989. Sparks and Prairie Fires: A Theory of Unanticipated Political Revolution. *Public Choice* 61:41–74.

Kuznets, Simon. 1966. *Modern Economic Growth*. New Haven: Yale University Press.

Lal, Deepak. 1983. *The Poverty of "Development Economic"*. London: Institute of Economic Affairs.

Lal, Deepak, and Sylvia Maxfield. 1993. The Political Economy of Stabilization in Brazil. In *Political and Economic Interactions in Economic Policy Reform,* edited by R. H. Bates and A. O. Krueger. Oxford: Blackwell.

Leakey, Louis S. B. 1977. *The Southern Kikuyu Before 1903*. 3 vols. London: Academic Press.

Leith, Clark, and Michael Lofchie. 1993. Structural Adjustment in Ghana. In *Political and Economic Interactions in Economic Policy Reform,* edited by R. H. Bates and A. O. Krueger. Oxford: Blackwell.

Levi, Margaret. 1981. The Predatory Theory of Rule. *Politics and Society* 10, no. 4:431–66.

———. 1988. *Of Rule and Revenue*. Berkeley and Los Angeles: University of California Press.

———. 1997. *Consent, Dissent, and Patriotism*. Chicago: University of Chicago Press.

Little, I. M. D. 1982. *Economic Development*. New York: Basic Books.

Little, I. M. D., Tibor Scitovsky, and Maurice Scott. 1970. *Industry and Trade in Some Developing Countries*. Oxford: Oxford University Press.

Londregan, John B. 2000. *Legislative Institutions in Chile*. Cambridge: Cambridge University Press.

MacCaffrey, Wallace T. 1961. Place and Patronage in Elizabethan Politics. In *Elizabethan Government and Society*, edited by S. T. Bindoff, J. Hurstfield, and C. H. Williams. London: University of London at the Athlone Press.

McCloskey, Deidre. 1985. *Applied Theory of Price*. New York: Macmillan.

McConnell, Grant. 1966. *Private Power and American Democracy*. New York: Knopf.

McFarlane, K. B. 1973. *The Nobility of Later Medieval Europe*. Oxford: Clarendon Press.

———. 1981. *England in the Fifteenth Century*. London: Hambledon Press.

McNeil, William. 1982. *The Pursuit of Power*. Chicago: University of Chicago Press.

Marx, Karl. 1906. *Capital*. New York: Modern Library.

———. 1978. The Eighteenth Brumaire of Louis Bonaparte. In *The Marx-Engels Reader*, ed. Robert C. Tucker. New York: W. W. Norton.

Maxfield, Sylvia. 1997. *Gatekeepers of Growth*. Princeton, N.J.: Princeton University Press.

Meek, Ronald. 1963. *The Economics of Physiocracy*. Cambridge: Cambridge University Press.

Meier, Gerald, and Dudley Seers, eds. 1984. *Pioneers of Development*. New York: Oxford University Press.

Meillassoux, Claude. 1981. *Maidens, Meal, and Money*. Cambridge: Cambridge University Press.

Meillassoux, Claude, ed. 1971. *The Development of Indigenous Trade and Markets in West Africa*. London: International Africa Institute Oxford University Press.

Mitchell, J. Clyde. 1956. *The Kalela Dance*. Manchester, Eng.: Rhodes-Livingstone Institute Manchester University Press.

Mitchell, S. K. 1951. *Taxation in Medieval Europe*. New Haven: Yale University Press.

Mitford, A. B., ed. 1966. *The Forty-seven Ronins: Tales of Old Japan*. Tokyo: Charles E. Tuttle.

Moore, Barrington. 1966. *Social Origins of Dictatorship and Democracy*. Boston: Beacon Press.

Moore, Mick. 1998. Death without Taxes: Democracy, State Capacity, and Aid Dependence in the Fourth World. In *The Democratic Development State: Politics and Institutional Design,* edited by M. Robinson and G. White. Oxford, Oxford University Press.

Mosley, Paul, Jane Harrington, and John Toye, eds. 1991. *Aid and Power*. 2 vols. New York and London: Routledge.

Mumford, Lewis. 1961. *The City in History*. New York: Harcourt Brace.

Njonjo, Apollo. 1977. The Africanization of the "White Highlands." Ph.D. diss. Princeton University.

North, Douglass C., and Robert Paul Thomas. 1973. *The Rise of the Western World*. Cambridge: Cambridge University Press.

North, Douglass C., and Barry R. Weingast. 1989. Constitutions and Commitment. *Journal of Economic History*. 69:803–32.

O'Donnell, Guillermo, and Philippe C. Schmitter. 1986. *Tentative Conclusions*. Vol. 5 of *Transitions from Authoritarian Rule*. Baltimore: The Johns Hopkins University Press.

Ormrod, David. 1985. *English Grain Exports and the Structure of Agrarian Capitalism, 1700–1760*. Hull, Eng.: Hull University Press.

Ormrod, W. M. 1990. *The Reign of Edward III*. New Haven: Yale University Press.

Outhwaite, R. B. 1981. Dearth and Government Intervention in English Grain Markets, 1590–1700. *Economic History Review* 34:389–406.

Paige, Jeffrey. 1997. *Coffee and Power*. Cambridge, Mass.: Harvard University Press.

Parsons, J. J. 1949. *Antioqueño Colonization in Western Columbia*. Berkeley and Los Angeles: University of California Press.

Peck, Linda Levy. 1990. *Court Patronage and Corruption in Early Stuart England*. Boston: Unwin Hyman.

Persson, Torsten, and Guido Tabellini, eds. 1994. *Politics*. Vol. 2 of *Monetary and Fiscal Policy*. Cambridge, Mass.: MIT Press.

Pirenne, Henri. 1968. Commerce Creates Towns. In *Town Origins*, edited by J. Benton. Boston: Heath.

Polanyi, Karl. 1944. *The Great Transformation*. Boston: Beacon Press.

Pollard, A. F. 1926. *The Evolution of Parliament*. London: Longman.

Popkin, Samuel L. 1979. *The Rational Peasant*. Berkeley and Los Angeles: University of California Press.

Prestwich, Michael. 1972. *War, Politics and Finance under Edward I*. London: Faber and Faber.

Przeworski, Adam. 1991. *Democracy and Markets*. Cambridge: Cambridge University Press.

Putnam, Robert. 1993. *Making Democracy Work*. Princeton, N.J.: Princeton University Press.

Putterman, Louis, ed. 1986. *The Economic Nature of the Firm.* New York: Oxford University Press.

Redfield, Robert. 1973. *Tepoztlan.* Chicago: University of Chicago Press.

Reno, William. 1995. *Corruption and State Politics in Sierra Leone.* Cambridge: Cambridge University Press.

———. 1998. *Warlord Politics and African States.* Boulder, Colo.: Lynne Rienner.

Rimmer, Douglas. 1995. The Effect of Conflict II: Economic Effects. In *Conflict in Africa,* edited by O. Furley. London: I. B. Tauris.

Rogowski, Ronald. 1987. Trade and the Variety of Democratic Institutions. *International Organization.* 41, no. 2:203–33.

Root, Hilton. 1994. *The Fountain of Privilege: Political Foundations of Markets in Old Regime France and England.* Berkeley and Los Angeles: University of California Press.

Rosenthal, Jean-Laurent. 1998. The Political Economy of Absolutism Reconsidered. In *Analytic Narratives,* edited by R. H. Bates, A. Greif, M. Levi, J.-L. Rosenthal, and B. R. Weingast. Princeton, N.J.: Princeton University Press.

Rothchild, Donald, ed. 1991. *Ghana: The Political Economy of Recovery.* Boulder, Colo.: Lynne Rienner.

Saboloff, Jeremy A., and C. C. Lamberg-Karlovsky. 1975. *Ancient Civilization and Trade.* Albuquerque: University of New Mexico Press.

Sachs, Jeffrey D., ed. 1989. *Developing Country Debt and the World Economy.* Chicago: National Bureau of Economic Research University of Chicago Press.

Sahlins, Marshal D. 1961. The Segmentary Lineage: An Organization of Predatory Expansion. *American Anthropologist.* 63:322–45.

———. 1968. *Tribesmen.* Englewood Cliffs, N.J.: Prentice-Hall.

Saul, Mahir. 1993. Land Custom in Bare: Agnatic Cooperation and Rural Capitalism in Western Burkino. In *Land in African Agrarian Systems,* edited by T. J. Bassett and D. E. Crummy. Madison, Wisc.: University of Wisconsin Press.

Schatzberg, Michael. 1988. *The Dialectics of Oppression in Zaire.* Bloomington, Ind.: Indiana University Press.

———. 1991. *Mobutu or Chaos?* Lanham, Md.: University Press of America.

Schultz, Theodore W. 1976. *Transforming Traditional Agriculture*. New York: Arno Press.

Scott, James C. 1976. *The Moral Economy of the Peasant*. New Haven: Yale University Press.

Scott, James C., and Benedict J. Tria Kerkvliet. 1986. *Everyday Forms of Peasant Resistance in South Asia*. Totowa, N.J.: Frank Cass.

Sheppard, Francis. 1998. *London: A History*. Oxford: Oxford University Press.

Skidmore, Thomas. 1967. *Politics in Brazil, 1930–1964*. New York: Oxford University Press.

Skocpol, Theda. 1979. *States and Social Revolutions*. Cambridge: Cambridge University Press.

Smith, Adam. 1976. *An Inquiry into the Nature and Causes of the Wealth of Nations*, edited by E. Cannan. Chicago: University of Chicago Press.

Soskice, David, Robert H. Bates, and David Epstein. 1992. Ambition and Constraint: The Stabilizing Role of Institutions. *Journal of Law, Economics, and Organizations* 8, no. 3:547–60.

Stallings, Barbara, and Philip Brock. 1993. Economic Adjustment in Chile. In *Economic and Political Interactions in Economic Policy Reform*, edited by R. H. Bates and A. O. Krueger. Oxford: Blackwell.

Stone, Lawrence. 1965. *The Crisis of the Aristocracy, 1558–1641*. Oxford: Clarendon Press.

———. 1973. *Family and Fortune*. Oxford: Clarendon Press.

Sturzenegger, Federico, and Mariano Tommasi, eds. 1998. *The Political Economy of Reform*. Cambridge, Mass.: MIT Press.

Swainson, Nicola. 1979. *The Development of Corporate Capitalism in Kenya*. Berkeley and Los Angeles: University of California Press.

Tilly, Charles. 1975. Reflections on the History of State Making. In *The Formation of Nation States in Western Europe*, edited by C. Tilly. Princeton, N.J.: Princeton University Press.

Time (Asia), May 24, 1999.

Tirole, Jean. 1989. *The Theory of Industrial Organization*. Cambridge, Mass.: MIT Press.

Todaro, Michael. 1994. *Economic Development in the Third World*. New York: Longman.

Trimberger, Ellen Kay. 1978. *Revolution from Above*. New Brunswick, N.J.: Transaction.

Turner, Ralph V. 1994. *King John*. New York: Longman.

Uchendu, Victor C. 1965. *The Igbo of Southeast Nigeria*. New York: Holt, Rinehart and Winston.

van Creveld, Martin L. 1977. *Supplying War: Logistics from Wallenstein to Patton*. Cambridge: Cambridge University Press.

van de Walle, Nicholas. Forthcoming. *The Politics of Permanent Crisis: Managing African Economies, 1979–1999*. New York: Cambridge University Press.

van Velsen, J. 1974. *The Politics of Kinship*. Manchester, Eng.: Institute of African Studies Manchester University Press.

Viner, Jacob. 1991. *Essays on the Intellectual History of Economics*. Princeton, N.J.: Princeton University Press.

Wade, Robert. 1990. *Governing the Market*. Princeton, N.J.: Princeton University Press.

Waltz, Kenneth. 1979. *The Theory of International Politics*. New York: McGraw-Hill.

Wantchekon, Leonard. 1996. *Political Coordination and Democratic Stability*. New Haven: Department of Political Science, Yale University.

Ward, Jennifer C. 1992. *English Noblewomen in the Later Middle Ages*. London: Longman.

Waugh, Scott L. 1988. *The Lordship of England: Royal Wardship and Marriage in English Society and Politics, 1217–1327*. Princeton, N.J.: Princeton University Press.

Weber, Max. 1958. Politics as a Vocation. In *From Max Weber*, edited by H. H. Gerth and C. W. Mills. New York: Oxford University Press.

———. 1968. *The City*. Translated by Don Martindale and Gertrud Neuwirth. New York: Free Press.

Weingast, Barry R. 1995. The Economic Role of Political Institutions. *The Journal of Law, Economics, and Organization* 7, no. 1: 1–31.

Werbner, Richard. 1993. From Heartland to Hinterland: Elites and the Geopolitics of Land in Botswana. In *Land in African Agrarian Systems*, edited by T. J. Bassett and D. E. Crummy. Madison, Wisc.: University of Wisconsin Press.

Wharton, Clifton. 1971. Risk, Uncertainty, and the Subsistence

Farmer. In *Economic Development and Social Change*, edited by G. Dalton. Garden City, N.Y.: Natural History Press.

Wilbur, Charles K., ed. 1973. *The Political Economy of Development and Underdevelopment*. New York: Random House.

Willard, J. F. 1934. *Parliamentary Taxation of Personal Property 1290 to 1334*. Cambridge, Mass.: Medieval Academy of America.

Williamson, Oliver E. 1985. *The Economic Institutions of Capitalism*. New York: Free Press.

Winsome, Leslie. 1993. *Zaire*. Boulder, Colo.: Westview.

Wolff, Eric R. 1966. *Peasants*. Englewood Cliffs, N.J.: Prentice-Hall.

World Bank. 1993. *The East Asian Miracle*. New York: Oxford University Press.

Woude, Ad van der, Akira Hayami, and Jan de Vries. 1990. *Urbanization in History: A Process of Dynamic Interactions*. New York: Oxford University Press.

Zartman, I. William. 1995. *Collapsed States*. Boulder, Colo.: Lynne Rienner.

INDEX